Managing and Raising Money that is Not Your Own:
Financial Management and Fundraising
in Non-Profit Organizations

Managing and Raising Money that is Not Your Own:
Financial Management and Fundraising in Non-Profit Organizations

by Ted Zerwin, MSW

Associate Clinical Professor
Josef Korbel School of International Studies
University of Denver

Vollie —
It's been good getting
to know you. All the best — always!
Ted

VANDEPLAS PUBLISHING
UNITED STATES OF AMERICA

Managing and raising money that is not your own: financial management and fundraising in non-profit organizations

Zerwin, Ted

Published by:

Vandeplas Publishing - July 2009

801 International Parkway, 5th Floor
Lake Mary, FL. 32746
USA

www.vandeplaspublishing.com

ISBN: 978-1-60042-079-5

DEDICATION

To an unbelievably wonderful lady named Su,

my wife of 40 years

TABLE OF CONTENTS

Page

Preface   ix

Introduction   1

Part A: Managing Money that is Not Your Own   3

Chapter 1: **Let's Lick Arthritis:** Why Non-Profit Organizations?   7

Chapter 2: **It Doesn't Make Sense:** Governance and Management   13
             of Non-Profit Organizations

Chapter 3: **Put Your Money Where Your Mouth Is:** Budgeting   23
             in Non-Profit Organizations

Chapter 4: **My Gut Tells Me It's Okay:** Financial Reporting   41
             In Non-Profit Organizations

Chapter 5: **She Has Ruined My Business:** Controlling Financial   55
             Operations in Non-Profit Organizations

Chapter 6: **Let's Save the Organization:** Taxes and Some Related   69
             Issues in Non-Profit Organizations

Part B: Raising Money that is Not Your Own   79

Chapter 7: **I Don't Like to Beg:** A Conceptual Approach to Fundraising 83
             in Non-Profit Organizations

Chapter 8: **But It's Just Junk Mail:** Annual Giving, Direct Mail,   103
             Internet, and Other Basic Fundraising Methods in
             Non-Profit Organizations

Chapter 9: **But a Lot of People Came:** Special Events in   121
         Non-Profit Organizations

Chapter 10: **They Let Me Put Our Names on a Building:** Major Gifts   137
         in Non-Profit Organizations

Chapter 11: **Call My Attorney and Trust Officer:** Bequests and   157
         Planned Giving in Non-Profit Organizations

Chapter 12: **What's in it For Us?** Corporate Fundraising in   169
         Non-Profit Organizations

Chapter 13: **When You Know One Foundation:** Grant Writing in   179
         Non-Profit Organizations

Epilogue   191

PREFACE

The origin of this book is my perceived need for it, following a career of almost 40 years working in non-profit charitable organizations, with 25 of those years as the President and CEO of the Rocky Mountain Chapter of the Arthritis Foundation, and after 12 years of teaching a course in "Financial Management and Fundraising in Non-Profit Organizations" in two Graduate Schools at the University of Denver. (These are the Graduate School of Social Work and the Josef Korbel School of International Studies.) When I began the staff leadership of the Arthritis Foundation back in 1976, I learned quickly that two highly important responsibilities would be financial management and fundraising. At the same time, I also knew that I had little if any education or experience in either discipline. As a result, I scurried around attempting to educate myself quickly in these topical areas. But I could not find a single source for the knowledge I needed. I found information on accounting for financial management and information on sales for fundraising. But these sources were quite different (Accountants and salespeople are not the same kind of people after all!) and didn't have the perspective I needed as an executive to not necessarily **do** both activities, but more often to **supervise and manage** them.

I experienced the same frustration when I was asked to begin teaching at the University of Denver. I could not find a single textbook on both financial management and fundraising for non-profit organizations. I found plenty on non-profit accounting, but they were too detailed for my students who were destined perhaps to be managers of accountants and needed to know how to read and understand budgets and financial reports, but not necessarily how to do them. I also found a lot of books on fundraising, but either they delved too specifically into only one or two areas of fundraising or they were so comprehensive that they provided much more knowledge than my students needed at the time. Therefore, I ended up requiring my graduate students to purchase and read two textbooks, both of which were too comprehensive and in depth for their needs and, of course, more expensive than they needed to be.

Thus, the idea for this book was born. I concluded that a book was needed, which not only combined the topics of financial management and fundraising, but also that was written with the perspective of someone who is now or will be required to understand, establish, supervise, and oversee these functions in a charitable organization – but **not** necessarily have to actually **do** them more than to a limited degree. I concluded, as well, that such a book would be valuable not only for my graduate students and for my executive and management colleagues in non-profit charitable organizations, but also for members of the Boards of Directors of these organizations. They, too, need the same perspective. They, too, need to understand, establish, and oversee these two functions in their organizations and not actually do them – except, of course, to a limited degree. In fact, one can make the case that these two functions are the most important ones for a Board of Directors to oversee among all of their responsibilities.

I chose the primary title for the book very carefully. I believe that **"Managing and Raising Money that is Not Your Own"** precisely reflects the perspective that a Staff Executive, Staff Manager, and Board Member need to have to carry out their fiduciary responsibility as a leader in a non-profit charitable organization. I have often told my students that, during my years as a non-profit CEO, I felt much more responsibility for the finances of the organization than I did for my own. And it is right to feel this way! When generous people, at our request, entrust their hard earned dollars with us in the non-profit sector, they do so because they believe in the cause we represent and entrust us to do something about that cause. If we don't keep track of those dollars as accurately as possible and don't spend them for the specific reason for which they were given to us, then we violate that trust. And we (namely Board Members, Staff Managers, and Staff Executives) cannot blame anyone else in our organizations if this trust is violated. We are the responsible parties.

It is my sincere hope that the publication of this book provides students with the information they need in the areas of financial management and fundraising to undertake their cxareers in the management of non-profit charitable organizations. It is a meaningful and rewarding career (Mine certainly was!), and a good understanding and competence in these two areas are absolutely essential. I also hope that current Board Members, Staff Executives, and Staff Managers of non-profit organizations will find this book to be helpful as they carry out their important responsibilities. People's lives and well-being depend upon what you do everyday. These people trust you. Generous people, corporations, and foundations are giving you funds everyday to carry out your respective missions. They also trust you. I know that you do not want to violate that trust. Understanding and competence in financial management and fundraising are absolutely essential for you, too.

Before getting into the formal text, I wish to make three acknowledgements. The first is to the Arthritis Foundation, both in the Rocky Mountain region and throughout the United States. I've spent over 25 years being associated with this wonderful organization and its wonderful people, both staff and volunteers. Most of what I've learned about non-profit financial management and fundraising and what has been written here, I've learned from this organization and these people. I am most grateful.

Secondly, I want to acknowledge my graduate students at the University of Denver, both in the Josef Korbel School of International Studies and in the Graduate School of Social Work. They have inspired me to write this book in the first place. They constantly encouraged me along the way. And, most of all, they give me hope everyday that our world **will be** a better place. Their idealism, competence, and energy **will** make a difference. I am most grateful.

Finally, I owe my daughter, Sarah, a lot. She has edited this text for me every step of the way. In the process, she has taught me how to write more precisely and clearly. She will soon have her Ph.D. in Education from the University of Colorado and continues to be a terrific high school teacher. Besides, she is one terrific daughter, wife, and mother! I am most grateful.

INTRODUCTION

This is a very practical book. As stated in the preface, its primary audience is three-fold, namely, (1) students preparing for careers in the management of non-profit charitable organizations, (2) current staff executive and administrative leaders of non-profit organizations, and (3) current volunteer members of the Boards of Directors of these organizations. These distinct groups of people share a common practical need, which is that they all will or now have the important responsibility to oversee the financial management and fundraising programs of non-profit organizations, but not necessarily to actually perform these functions, at least to any great degree. I believe that this book provides the precise practical information required to respond to this common practical need.

The book is full of real-life examples largely drawn from my long professional and executive career in the management of non-profit organizations, especially in my role as the President and CEO of the Arthritis Foundation, Rocky Mountain Chapter. This career has given me the opportunity to not only learn a lot about financial management and fundraising, but also, mostly after trial and error, to determine good policies and practices to put into place to achieve the goals of sound financial management and effective fundraising. I make no claims beyond the fact that the policies and practices recommended in this book are indeed "good" and have worked for me and the organization I led. The reader will have to decide if they will apply to the particular organization with which he or she is affiliated or may be affiliated. But I believe strongly that the policies and practices outlined here definitely apply and will work for all kinds of non-profit charitable organizations.

Why does this book have applicability beyond the particular circumstances and environments of my professional and executive career? There are at least two significant reasons for this applicability. First, and perhaps most importantly, all non-profit charitable organizations share much more in common than they do not. Their primary differences are found in their specific missions, goals, and activities. But they are very similar in the ways that they are generally organized, governed, financed, and staffed to carry out their divergent – and sometimes even contradictory – missions, goals, and activities. For example, a non-profit, faith-based pregnancy counseling organization and a non-sectarian organization in the same field of work may be offering very different and oftentimes contradictory mission-focused services, while at the same time they implement similar financial management and fundraising practices. In a similar manner, a small community center located in a low income area of the city and a high visibility community arts organization in the same city, while they may have vastly different budgets, styles of operation, and people involved on their respective Boards, will have to put into operation the same basic financial management and fundraising procedures if they are to achieve their very divergent missions.

The second reason for the applicability of the policies and practices advocated in this book beyond the specific parameters of my professional career is that I have concluded to these recommendations only after much reading and learning about the practices of many different kinds of organizations, after many conversations with executive colleagues in other organizations, and after following advice of many board members over the years who have experiences in different organizations.

With these thoughts in mind, throughout the text, even though there is a preponderance of examples drawn from my own career, I have tried very hard to state the recommended policies and practices in ways that can apply to all non-profit charitable organizations – of all sizes and budgets, with divergent missions and goals, and operating in varying social, political, geographic, and economic environments.

The book is divided into two parts. Part A, entitled "Managing Money that is Not Your Own" and containing six chapters, discusses financial management in the context of three basic principles, namely, accountability, transparency, and fiduciary responsibility, and shows how these principles can best be applied in the practical order. Part B, entitled "Raising Money that is Not Your Own" and having seven chapters, presents a comprehensive fundraising program that has as its foundation a strong base of individual givers and discusses all methods of charitable giving.

PART A: **MANAGING MONEY THAT IS NOT YOUR OWN**

I frequently tell my graduate students at the University of Denver that good financial management is more important in the non-profit charitable organization sector than in the for-profit sector because much more is at stake. In other words, when a for-profit venture goes out of business, investors lose money and employees may lose their jobs, but consumers are usually not affected at all. They can go somewhere else to purchase their hamburgers, hardware items, or whatever else is involved. However, when a non-profit charitable organization goes out of business, the consumers or clients are usually affected significantly. They may have nowhere else to go. And, when non-profits go out of business, it's rare that the cause is that their programs are not needed. Rather, the reason for the default is usually financial in nature. The Boards of Directors and executive staffs of the affected organizations have simply not practiced good financial management.

This should be reason enough to motivate us to practice good financial management in our non-profit charitable organizations. But recently another important factor has raised its ugly head. There is growing evidence to suggest that many government leaders and staff members of non-profit organizations are questioning the integrity and ethical standards of the non-profit sector. Articles in <u>The Chronicle of Philanthropy</u>, a bi-weekly newspaper that monitors the ups and downs in the non-profit sector in the United States, introduce this topic very well. A first quote focuses on the questioning of government leaders:

> Lawmakers are preparing to introduce an ambitious legislative package that they say could alter the nonprofit world more than any government action in the past three decades.
>
> For more than a year, as U.S. senators and their aides have delved into abuses they have seen in the nonprofit world, they have spoken with hundreds of charity and foundation leaders

and read thousands of pages of documents detailing how changes they seek could hurt charities.

Last week, at the second Senate Finance Committee hearing on the subject in the past 10 months, Internal Revenue Service Commissioner Mark W. Everson raised the stakes in the fight to curb nonprofit abuses when he told lawmakers that indiscretions by nonprofit groups and donors are costing the federal government about $15-billion a year in lost revenue.

At the hearing, senators took aim at charities and foundations that pay excessive salaries to their executives, donors who write off bogus amounts on their taxes for noncash gifts, and wealthy people who bilk the tax system by using nonprofit organizations as a front to help pay for their personal expenses........

"There are increasing indications that the twin cancers of technical manipulation and outright abuse that we saw develop in the profit-making segments of the economy are now spreading to pockets of the nonprofit sector," Mr. Everson said. (1)

A second quote reflects the findings of a recent study among non-profit organization employees:

Nonprofit organizations have long held a reputation for having significantly higher ethical standards than businesses and government.

But a report released today by the Ethics Resource Center in Washington shows that gap is closing quickly – as standards at charities are declining at what the study's authors say is a disturbing rate.

Rates of observed misconduct at nonprofit organizations are at the highest level since the Ethics Resource Center began measuring in 2000. In 2007, more than half – 55 percent – of nonprofit employees observed one or more acts of misconduct in the previous year........

The frequency of these behaviors mirrors the frequency reported
in the for-profit and government arenas, the study found. (2)

Having worked in the non-profit sector for my total professional career and having nothing but respect for the staff and volunteer leaders I have found there, I am amazed and disturbed at the depth of mistrust and negative thinking about the non-profit sector in the United States, as exhibited by these quotes and many other similar ones that seem to be in such prevalence these days.

The important question is: Why? Why is there such mistrust and negative thinking? Part of the answer is most probably a general feeling in our society that many institutions are not trustworthy. Another part of the answer flows from the current negativity about corporate, for-profit America, caused by the many accounting and compensation scandals that have surfaced lately and, of course, by the faulty financial practices that have led to the current, severe economic downturn. But we in the non-profit sector are part of the answer, too. It's that part of the answer that we need to be concerned about. We can do something about that.

What are we in the non-profit sector doing – or not doing – to warrant such criticism? There are any number of plausible answers to this question. But let's focus on just three. The first concerns our **accountability** for the funds and other assets given to us to carry out our organizational missions. Being accountable means that we accept responsibility for the proper safekeeping, investment, and expenditure of the funds and other assets that we have. The Boards of Directors and executive staffs of the non-profit organizations that I have known do acknowledge and accept their financial management responsibilities. But the concern is that too often the responsibility is not shared <u>throughout</u> the organization. In other words, many Board members and staff leave the responsibility "to others" whom they judge to be more qualified to carry it out. This abdication of responsibility becomes particularly dangerous when, for example, the Board tends to "trust" the staff to make appropriate financial management decisions without oversight or when only a few "key" directors and/or staff make most of the financial decisions. Therefore, the goal is for all Board members and staff throughout the organization to share the responsibility for financial management. Everyone needs to truly feel this responsibility in accordance with his or her position within the organization.

The second issue is **transparency**. Being transparent means that our financial decisions, records and reports are made available to all who have a need or a legitimate desire to have the information. Again, the ideal of transparency is readily accepted in general by most non-profit organizations, but too often exceptions are made for apparently good reasons. In other words, we oftentimes question if a Board member, staff person, donor, client, or other interested person really "needs to know." Indeed, there are instances when some financial information is rightly kept confidential from some people, for example, when specific salary information is not shared openly. But such instances are rare. The goal of transparency, therefore, is to share financial information with all interested people, both within and outside the organization. Why would we want to hide this information anyway?

The third and perhaps the most important issue is **fiduciary responsibility**. A fiduciary is a person or institution that is entrusted with the funds or assets of others. Non-profit organizations are fiduciaries in a very literal sense. This is especially clear when we accept charitable contributions or government and foundation grants to carry out our stated missions. The donors of the contributions and grants "trust" that we will use them efficiently, effectively, and even ethically for the purposes for which they are given. My experience tells me that non-profit organizations are generally trustworthy in this sense. But, for some reason, as was clear from the quotes that began this discussion, many governmental leaders, other members of the public, and members of our own staffs do not trust us. Our goal, therefore, in carrying out this fiduciary responsibility is to make our financial decisions with such accountability and transparency and to focus on our missions so well that no one can have any reason to doubt our trustworthiness.

The concepts of accountability, transparency, and fiduciary responsibility are clearly interrelated. Yet each principle is important on its own, in that it looks at the same reality from a different perspective. These concepts, individually and together, will permeate my total presentation on "Managing Money." My objective is to introduce readers to a financial management system that effectively employs all three concepts. I am convinced that financial practices, that are guided by these principles, will not only enable us in the non-profit charitable world to maintain our important status in this country, but also, and more significantly, to keep us in business and enable us to grow to meet the real needs of the clients we serve.

(1) Brad Wolverton, "Taking Aim at Charities," The Chronicle of Philanthropy, April 14, 2005, p. 27.

(2) Peter Panepento, "Ethical Standards Erode at Nonprofit Groups, Study Finds," The Chronicle of Philanthropy, March 27, 2008, Internet Report.

Chapter 1: Let's Lick Arthritis:

Why Non-Profit Organizations?

In New York City in 1948, Floyd Odlum, the CEO of the Johnson & Johnson Corporation, met with four doctors from across the United States to discuss the need for an organization to raise funds to expand research into arthritis and other rheumatic diseases. The five complained that not enough research was being done and concluded that, just as for cancer there was the Cancer Society and for heart disease there was the Heart Association, a non-profit organization for arthritis was needed. So they agreed to start the Arthritis Foundation by returning to their own communities and recruiting additional volunteers. They planned to meet again soon with additional people and to formally organize at that time. In the meantime, Mr. Odlum suggested that the goal of their efforts could be stated simply: "Let's Lick Arthritis!" The Arthritis Foundation still exists today, with the same dedication of those five founders and with a mission statement that, although greater in length, carries the same spirit and intent.

This story, taken from the annals on the Arthritis Foundation and passed down to new volunteers as they are recruited year after year, illustrates something interesting and perhaps wonderful in the history of the United States – the non-profit or third sector. This chapter will present the historical rationale of and describe the non-profit sector as it now exists in the following manner. First, I will present an historical and conceptual introduction to the third sector. Then, I will list and describe the many different kinds of non-profit organizations. Third, I will narrow the focus to the subject matter of this text, namely, to organizations that have the IRS classification of 501(c)(3). Finally, I will point out the similarities and differences between non-profit charitable organizations and those that function under for-profit and governmental auspices.

The Third Sector

From the beginnings of this country, citizens concluded that they could not expect governmental systems to meet all their needs. So, when needs were identified that were not being met enough by government or not at all, oftentimes groups of citizens formed organizations around these needs. The new organizations were not sponsored by government, and they were not run to make a profit. Thus, the "Third Sector" was born, to distinguish it from both government and business. Such organizations, called non-profits, now exist in almost every field imaginable: health, social service, education, the arts, humanities, athletics, the professions, youth, and the elderly. And now such voluntary efforts are beginning to catch on around the world in other countries, where they tend to be called "non-governmental organizations" or "NGO's." This Third Sector may very well be the United States' greatest gift to the world.

One can argue of course, both philosophically and politically, that the non-profit sector in the United States has become so large and so active that it has done a disservice to this country, in that it has assumed some responsibilities that rightly belong with government. This argument is advanced through comparison with other countries where government takes much more responsibility for the well-being of its citizens, especially in the health and social service fields, and by showing that the United States ranks 17th lowest in total taxation (29.6%) among countries in the industrialized world. (1) But I choose not to enter into this argument in this text, primarily because it is beyond the scope of this book. Rather, I choose to treat the non-profit or third sector as a given reality in the United States, through which much can be accomplished. The book also treats the sector as a growing reality in other countries where groups of citizens are finding it to be an effective way to get important things done.

Over the years, the non-profit sector in the United States has grown in size and stature. Current Internal Revenue Service (IRS) statistics indicate that in 2006 there were 1,585,479 non-profit organizations of all kinds in the United States. This number represented a growth of 15,456 organizations over the year before. (2) Considering the facts that this sector not only employs a high number of paid staff but also millions of volunteers, there is no doubt that the sector has a tremendous impact on American society.

Kinds of Non-Profit Organizations

Non-profit organizations take many forms. Some are fraternal groups, like the Lions or Elks Clubs. Others represent professionals, such as the American Medical Association or the Board of Realtors. Others exist to serve the recreational needs of their members, like golf and tennis clubs or associations of runners. A large number operate educational or health institutions. Many function as churches or under religious auspices. Others are national in scope and represent large health interests, such as the American Heart and Diabetes Associations, and have local Chapters and Divisions. Some are concerned about human and civil rights, like the American Civil Liberties Union and Amnesty International. Many are only local in nature, such as community centers. Some promote business interests, like city and state Chambers of Commerce. Many provide needed services, like day care and youth programs. They can represent competing interests, like environmental groups and associations of oil companies. The possibilities are endless. But they all share many things in common. They all are in the Third Sector, that is, they are not government and not business; they do not operate for a profit; and they are run by Boards of Directors. They differ in their missions and by the differential tax status granted to them by the Internal Revenue Service (IRS).

501(c)(3) Organizations

The focus of this book is on those non-profit organizations that enjoy the most favorable tax status from the IRS and local taxing authorities. There were 1,064,191 of these charitable organizations in 2006 according to the IRS, and they represented 67.1% of all non-profit groups (3). The IRS categorizes these particular organizations as 501(c)(3). As such, they are not only exempt from most federal and local taxes. They also allow their contributors to take tax deductions for supporting them. This is clearly a huge advantage, not only over businesses, but also over other types of non-profit organizations. As a result, this tax status is more difficult to attain and, once attained, easier to lose. It is also more subject to governmental regulation.

The easiest way to understand the reasons behind the granting of a 501(c)(3) status to an organization is to look first at IRS regulations as contained in the actual Form 1023, which must be completed and submitted to the IRS before this tax status is granted. Form 1023 lists two "required provisions" for 501(c)(3) status. The first is that the articles of incorporation of the applicant group clearly state that the organization has an "exempt purpose(s), such as charitable, religious, educational, and/or scientific purposes." The second is that, if and when the organization dissolves, the "remaining assets must be used exclusively for exempt purposes, such as charitable, religious, educational, and/or scientific purposes." (4) Therefore, the intent of the IRS in granting this privileged tax status is clear. It will only recognize those organizations who operate solely for some charitable purpose, for some public good in other words, and not for the benefit of some few individuals. And this intent extends even to the potential dissolution of the organization, when any remaining assets must still go on supporting some public good. The ultimate reason why the IRS is so stingy in granting a 501(c)(3) status is the realization that the United States Treasury stands to lose income from the tax deductions of donors to such organizations.

But why does the U.S. Government allow these tax deductions? Built into the fabric of this country is the realization that non-profit charitable organizations are performing services for citizens that the government would otherwise have to provide. In other words, 501(c)(3) organizations enjoy a privileged status in this country. That is why the skepticism about charitable groups, mentioned in the introduction to Part A of this book, is such a great concern. We could lose this status. We could lose tax exemptions and the tax deductions of our donors. We could lose a large base of our support. That is why we need a financial management system that operates with accountability, transparency, and fiduciary responsibility.

Similarities and Differences with Business and Government

The final subject for this first chapter is how non-profit charitable organizations are similar to and different from business and government. The first point to make is that, in an operational sense, all three sectors are much more alike than different. To achieve their objectives, organizations in all three sectors must have strong executive leadership, sound management practices, good personnel management, responsiveness to the needs of the people they serve, positive public images, and efficient and effective operations. They must function as "good businesses" as this expression is commonly understood.

The differences are evident elsewhere. What primarily distinguishes non-profit charitable groups from businesses is two-fold. The first involves **purpose.** The ultimate purpose of a business is to create a profit for its owners. As seen above, this cannot in any way be even part of the purpose of a 501(c)(3) organization. The second difference concerns the **Boards.** Members of business corporate Boards of Directors can be remunerated specifically for their Board service and usually are.

Members of non-profit corporate Boards of Directors, although they can be reimbursed for their actual related expenses, are not usually paid for their Board service, and most such organizations in fact prohibit any remuneration of this kind.

The difference between non-profit charitable organizations and government agencies is not quite as clear. They each have the same ultimate purpose – the public good. The difference is found at the policy level. Governmental agencies receive their policy direction from publicly elected officials and their appointees. Charitable groups receive their policy direction from privately elected or appointed Boards of Directors.

Other differences are more subtle, but perhaps just as important. As opposed to businesses, non-profit charitable groups tend to operate with a greater sense of mission, resulting in employees having feelings that they are contributing to the well-being of others. And working side-by-side with dedicated volunteers, almost never seen in the business world, increases these positive feelings. As opposed to governmental agencies, charitable organizations tend to operate with more flexibility and less procedure and regulation. They usually have many more volunteers, as well. There are exceptions to these differences, of course, and the differences are more a matter of style than substance. But they appear to be very real in most cases.

Bullet Summary

♦ The Third Sector, composed of non-profit organizations that are fundamentally different from business and government, has a strong historical base in the United States and carries out important missions in our society.

♦ Non-profit organizations are growing in numbers and influence around the world, primarily known as non-governmental organizations or NGO's.

♦ Non-profit organizations exist in almost every field, from social service to health, from professional associations to membership groups, and from business to recreation.

♦ Non-profit charitable organizations, representing about two-thirds of all non-profit groups, enjoy a preferential 501(c)(3) status from the IRS, which allows them to solicit and accept tax-deductible donations from the public and not pay taxes on their related income.

◆ Non-profit charitable organizations have this preferential status because of a societal belief that they perform valuable public services that otherwise would have to be provided by government.

◆ Non-profit charitable organizations, although they are structurally different and vary in style from organizations in the business and government sectors, still have many operational features in common with these other sectors.

Conclusion

The primary conclusions to draw from this first chapter are that non-profit charitable organizations perform vital functions in our society and are given preferential status to assist them in achieving their missions. Given the current skepticism about the integrity of these organizations, they must be governed and managed in ways to enhance and maintain the public trust. This leads to the subject matter of the next chapter.

(1) NationMaster.Com: "Total taxation as % of GDP by country."

(2) IRS statistics as summarized by The Chronicle of Philanthropy, April 5, 2007.

(3) Ibid.

(4) IRS Form 1023, p. 2

Suggested Readings

Blazek, IRS Form 1023 Tax Preparation Guide, John Wiley & Sons, New York, 2005.

Brinckerhoff, Mission Based Management: Leading your Not-for-Profit in the 21st Century, John Wiley & Sons, New York, 2000, pp. 11-26.

Konrad and Novak, Financial Management for Non-Profits: Keys to Success, Regis University, Denver, 2004, pp.1-12.

McLaughlin, Streetsmart Financial Basics for Nonprofit Managers, John Wiley & Sons, New York, 2002, pp. 3-17.

Werther and Berman, Third Sector Management: The Art of Managing Nonprofit Organizations, Georgetown University Press, 2001, pp. 3-27.

Chapter 2: It Doesn't Make Sense:

Governance and Management of Non-Profit Organizations

Frequently, when I speak to graduate students in the classroom about the fact that Boards of Directors – and not staff – have the primary and ultimate responsibility for the continuing existence of non-profit organizations, a student or two will remark: "It doesn't make sense!" They make the remark in the context of the realization that Board members give only intermittent time to the organization – while staff members usually give full-time – and staff members know much more about the day-to-day operation of the organization than Board members do. I have to agree. Without a complete understanding of the reasons for this, it really doesn't make sense.

The intent of this chapter is to impart this "complete understanding" so that the reader will see that it, indeed, does "make sense" that non-profit charitable organizations are governed and managed the way they are. First, I will explain that these organizations function as corporations, with all the legal implications that this term implies. Then, I will discuss the fundamental role played by a Board of Directors in the governance and policy making of an organization. Third, I will talk about the role of paid staff in a non-profit organization, giving emphasis to equitable compensation practices. Fourth, I will present a strong case for what is essential – at least in my opinion – for the effective operation of a non-profit organization, namely, a real partnership between Board and staff. Finally, I will mention briefly the organizational stages that most non-profit groups tend to pass through and the implications of these stages.

Non-Profit Organizations as Corporations

Charitable non-profit organizations function as corporations in every legal sense. In fact, in the United States, these organizations cannot gain their 501(c)(3) status from the IRS until after they have filed their Articles of Incorporation with their respective State and received recognition from that State of official corporate status. And these Articles must be included, along with approved Bylaws, with the completed application Form 1023 to the IRS.

The Articles of Incorporation make up the founding document of the new non-profit organization. Information included is the organization's formal name, a description of its specific charitable purposes, a list of its incorporators, and other basic data. Of particular importance is a statement clearly indicating that the net earnings of the organization cannot inure to the benefit of directors, officers, or other private persons. Equally important is a declaration that, upon dissolution of the corporation, all remaining assets will be distributed to another 501(c)(3) organization. A helpful inclusion in recent years is a statement limiting the liability of individual directors within certain restrictions.

The Bylaws compose the operating document for the non-profit organization. They are usually longer and much more detailed than the Articles. Important information included is as follows: statement of purpose; definition of members (if any); numbers, terms, election, and rules of procedure for the Board of Directors; meetings, officers and committees of the Board; determination of the corporate fiscal year; and other significant items. The information about the Board of Directors is especially critical and must contain definitive statements that rules are in place to prevent conflict of interest in the Board's decision making and to disallow any compensation to Board members for their service.

The Articles and Bylaws tend to make for boring reading, but they are extremely important because they – together – establish the corporate identity and procedures for the non-profit charitable organization. For this reason, I encourage my students to ask for copies of both and to study them before accepting employment. (Wouldn't this impress a prospective employer?!) For the same reason, I give similar encouragement to volunteers before they accept nomination for election to Boards of Directors.

Boards of Directors

The best way to understand the role of a Board of Directors in a non-profit organization is to consider the fact that the members of a Board are the actual successors to the founders of the organization, no matter how old it may be. Those founders **were** the organization in the beginning, and, most probably, there were no staff involved at the time. In like manner, a current Board of Directors **is** the organization in the strict legal sense. It is the accountable group, and, as such, it has the responsibility for the governance, financial situation, policies, and, above all, the mission adherence of the corporation. This is so true that the Board members, both as a group and individually, are the likely targets of a suit against the organization.

Why is this the case? Why is the Board the ultimately accountable group, even though "it may not make sense" as stated above in the introduction to this chapter? The simple answer, of course, is the fact that corporate law says this is true. But this does not tell us why. The real answer is that a successful corporation must make good and objective decisions. And staff members, whose livelihood depends upon the financial success of the organization, are not in a position to make the good and objective decisions that are required. In other words, the best decisions may at times go against the self-interest of staff. On the other hand, the Board of Directors, both theoretically and really, is not supposed to have self-interest. Rather, it must base its decisions on what's best for the organization's mission and its clients.

I recently witnessed a real life example of this. A non-profit organization, just two weeks before the close of its fiscal year, learned that it could lose about $25,000 in surplus grant funds if it did not spend them for program activities by the end of the year. With this in mind, the staff brought a proposal to the Board to spend the total amount for staff bonuses. The Board agreed that this would be a legitimate use of the funds and that the staff was most deserving of this extra and unexpected remuneration, but, because several Board members knew the mind of the grantor very well, they stated that they were uncomfortable with all the surplus being spent in this way. They feared that this could damage the organization down the road and even jeopardize its future funding. So the Board excused the staff and went into executive session. After full discussion, the Board decided to instruct its Chair to inform the staff that half of the funds could be spent for bonuses, but that the other half would have to be spent for other program reasons or returned. Without a doubt, this was a "good and objective decision" for the future of the organization.

Realizing this ultimate accountability of the Board of Directors, several things are necessary to assure that the Board makes the best corporate decisions and to protect Board members from unwarranted legal tangles and personal expense. To assist in their corporate decision making, Board members must not only make it their business to study the issues, but they also must be given the benefit of the knowledge and opinions of staff who may very well know the issues better. To protect Board members from legal difficulties, most non-profit organizations in these days purchase Directors and Officers Insurance in their behalf and indemnify them in their Articles of Incorporation and Bylaws as much as the law allows.

Staff of Non-Profit Organizations

Stated simply and clearly, the staff of a non-profit organization works for the Board of Directors. In other words, its role is to carry out the policies and direction of the Board. This does not mean that the staff is a subservient group. Rather it means that it has a different role than the Board. In healthy organizations, staff members function in partnership with the Board. The next section of this chapter will describe ways in which the organization can best carry out this partnership. But there is more to say about a non-profit organization's staff.

There is no doubt that people who are paid to work in a non-profit charitable organization tend to have much more at stake than those working in the for-profit sector. They want meaningful work and fair compensation, and they share these desires with their for-profit colleagues. But, in addition, I have observed that they want to make a difference in their world. They want to go home at night knowing that they have made some contribution to the well-being of others. And, for this extra "compensation," they are oftentimes willing to forego some monetary compensation that they may have been able to receive in the for-profit sector.

Given the truth of this observation, it does not excuse Boards of Directors and staff executives from striving to compensate their staffs as fairly as possible, commensurate with the skills they bring and contributions they make. And, although non-profit charitable organizations may not be able to compensate at the level of the for-profit sector, they should be as competitive as possible in the marketplace, realizing that the retention of good staff requires it.

Staff compensation assumes special importance when it comes to that of the staff executive or President. In particular, the IRS monitors this very carefully in relation to the preservation of the organization's 501(c)(3) status. Related to this is the fact that the relatively high differential in compensation between executives and other employees in the for-profit sector is not accepted in the non-profit sector, either within the organizations themselves or by the public that supports them. So, in determining the compensation of its executive, the Board of the non-profit organization needs to be concerned about both external appropriateness and internal fairness.

In regard to external concerns, especially the IRS, the Board needs to assure itself that it has done sufficient study before it sets the compensation level of its executive. Most communities, through one umbrella organization or another, do salary surveys of non-profit executives and other management staff, based upon size of budget and staff and field of activity. Many national affiliate organizations do the same. The documented use of such survey information and setting salary ranges based upon that information provide ample evidence to the IRS and other watchdog agencies that a Board has been adequately conscientious in this important matter.

Internal fairness is another matter. A staff executive deserves a competitive compensation package, taking into consideration his or her qualifications, tenure, and performance. The salary surveys mentioned above are a great help in this regard. But looking at the executive's salary level, relative to the salaries of other staff in the same organization, is also an important consideration. Unfortunately in my opinion, according to a recent article in the <u>Chronicle of Philanthropy</u>, there is a "growing disparity" between the salaries of staff executives and other workers in non-profit organizations. (1) If this disparity is considered to be unfair in the minds of other staff – and other staff members **know** what the executive is paid, regardless of how hard the organization tries to keep this information confidential – it can cause some severe morale problems. The same is true for volunteers, regular donors, and even clients. The Board must feel comfortable that it has satisfied the concerns of all of these groups and that the salary level is truly defensible. What is a guideline in this regard? That's a hard question, especially because no such guideline appears to exist. Perhaps a start is that the executive should not be compensated at more than twice the level of other high level staff and not more than five times the level of the least compensated in the organization. I offer these proposed guidelines as a way to at least get the discussion started in the field.

The Board-Staff Partnership

I stated above that Board and staff play different roles in a non-profit organization. The Board's role is to establish the policies for the organization and to determine its overall direction. The staff's role is to implement those policies in accordance with the direction that the Board has set. Another simple way to say the same thing is to say that the Board deals with the "what," and the staff deals with the "how." All in the organization must clearly understand this role difference and make it operational. Otherwise confusion and even resentment on all sides can result.

I have often witnessed an interesting phenomenon in this regard. When a Board perceives that it has "weak" staff leadership, it easily rushes into the implementation side of the operation. Likewise, when the staff perceives that it has a "weak" Board, it strives to gain and maintain control of organization policies. This is a most natural thing to happen, because the "strong" partner concludes that it must overstep its bounds if the organization is to attain its mission. In some instances, this may be a necessary step in the short run. But, over a longer time, the resulting resentment and confusion can easily destroy the organization or at least make it ineffective.

All this being said, there is much room for crossover in the practical order. For example, an intelligent Board of Directors certainly consults with its staff, especially its executive, before it makes important policy decisions. In like manner, individual Board members, based upon their interests and skills, may assist in the implementation of policies and programs, either formally through committees or informally. When Board members "roll up their sleeves and get to work" in this way, it usually results in increased harmony and effectiveness in the organization. In both instances described in this paragraph, the Board-staff partnership becomes very real.

The key to the development of an effective Board-staff partnership is an appropriate conceptual understanding of the roles of the Board Chair and Staff Executive or President, as illustrated by Figure 1. The Board of Directors makes two overriding decisions in its desire to achieve its mission and to make sure that the organization implements its policies. First, it elects a Chair of the Board and gives him or her full responsibility for management of the volunteer side of the operation, including the appointment and supervision of all committee chairs. Second, it hires a Staff Executive or President and gives him or her full responsibility for management of the staff side of the operation, including the hiring and supervision of all other staff members. Notice in Figure 1 that there are solid lines from the Board to the Chair and President and then to the committee chairs and staff who function under their respective authority. These solid lines represent accountability in the strict sense. So, if the volunteer side of the organization is not functioning properly, the Board elects a new Chair. Likewise, if the staff side of the operation is not functioning properly, the Board hires a new President.

It is also important to note the broken lines between the volunteer and staff sides of the operation. In effective organizations, there are all kinds of inter-relationships between volunteers and staff as they work together to fulfill the mission. **But** these broken lines do not represent accountability. They only represent cooperative relationships that are necessary for success.

Figure 1
Accountability in Non-Profit Charitable Organizations

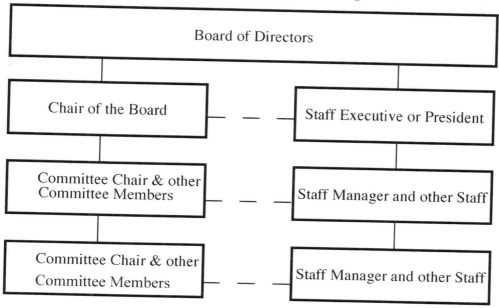

In the practical order, if there is a real partnership between the Chair of the Board and Staff Executive, the chances are good that this sense of partnership will permeate throughout the whole organization. This can be a challenge, especially because there is regular turnover in the Chair position, while the Staff Executive tends to be a more permanent fixture. In my experience, the transition to a new Chair of the Board was always a critical moment. Every Chair is different, and he or she brings different skills and personal goals to the position. In my opinion, it is the Staff Executive's responsibility to become aware of these differences and to take the initiative in the establishment of a good working partnership with the new Chair. Thus, these two key leaders can truly "fill each other's gaps" as they lead the organization.

There is one final thought about the Board-staff partnership. I feel strongly that regular Board meetings should be open to the attendance of all staff in small organizations and to all key staff in large organizations. It is good for the staff to witness the Board, its employer, in action and to be able to communicate formally and informally with individual Board members or with the Board as a whole. It is also good for the Board to become acquainted with all staff members and to seek their counsel as it makes important decisions. Obviously, there are times when the Board may need to have some deliberations without staff present or only with the Staff Executive present, but Board meetings that are open to staff on a regular basis will enhance organizational effectiveness.

Organizational Stages

Many authors in the non-profit field (2) have noted that organizations tend to go through various stages and, as they do, the relationship between Board and staff needs to adapt to the new situation. First, there is a **beginning** stage of the organization in which the Board usually takes a very active role, not only in policy, but also in implementation, because there may be few or no staff at all. Second, there is the **developing** stage in which the Board and staff work together to establish growth and stability in the organization. Third, there is the stage of **maturity**, when the organization has become fully developed and can look to the future with confidence, with both Board and staff concentrating almost exclusively only on their respective responsibilities. The time involved in passing through these stages varies from organization to organization, but most often there are at least several years involved. In addition, a particular organization may revert to a previous stage due to special circumstances.

As the organization moves through these phases, the Board itself needs to be sensitive to the ways in which the organization carries out its work and be willing to change its focus as the staff becomes stronger and more capable of carrying out its responsibilities. Equally important is the fact that the Board must choose both volunteer and staff leaders who are appropriate for each stage of the organization's life. And the Board and staff leaders themselves must adapt to the requirements of each transition and change their modes of operation as needed.

Bullet Summary

◆ Non-profit charitable organizations are corporations in the strict sense, operating under the formal structure provided by Articles of Incorporation and Bylaws.

◆ The Board of Directors has the indispensable role of setting policies and direction for the organization. As a result, the Board – not the staff – is the ultimately accountable group for the organization.

◆ The staff of an organization is employed by the Board to carry out its policies in accordance with the overall direction it has set.

♦ The Board should compensate its staff as competitively as possible, conscious of being internally fair and sensitive to the external concerns of the IRS and the public.

♦ Board and staff need to work together to establish an effective partnership in the day-to-day operation of the organization. Key to this partnership is the working relationship between the Chair of the Board and the Staff Executive or President.

♦ Non-profit charitable organizations go through distinct phases: beginning, developing, and maturity. As these transitions take place, the Board and staff leadership needs to adapt and to change.

Conclusion

Of primary importance in this chapter is the fact the both Board and staff, even though they have distinct roles, need each other to achieve the mission of the non-profit charitable organization and to maintain its accountability. Their real partnership is absolutely essential. Nowhere is this more apparent than when the organization allocates its resources through the budgetary process to attain its goals. That is the subject of the next chapter.

(1) Harvey Lipman, "A Growing Disparity: Gap between pay for CEO's and workers is getting bigger," Chronicle of Philanthropy, November 10, 2005, pp. 26-31

(2) See, for example, Konrad & Novak, Financial Management for Nonprofits: Keys to Success, Regis University, 2000, pp.15-16, and Werther & Berman, Third Sector Management: The Art of Managing Nonprofit Organizations, Georgetown University Press, 2001, pp. 7-11.

Suggested Readings

Brinckeroff, op.cit., pp. 50-100.

Konrad and Novak, op.cit., pp. 13-26.

Werther and Berman, op.cit., pp. 51-114

Chapter 3: Put Your Money Where Your Mouth Is:

Budgeting in Non-Profit Organizations

Many times during my long career with the Arthritis Foundation, we would tell people with arthritis and donors that our highest priority was supporting medical research in order to solve the major health problem of arthritis and to eventually go out of business when this was accomplished. This two-fold statement was wonderfully idealistic, not at all unlike the public statements made by many other charitable organizations, and we really meant it. Moreover, the statement was always received enthusiastically. But was it honest? It was only honest to the extent that these same clients and donors could look at our current budget and see that a significant amount of money was allocated to research in comparison to the amounts allocated to other programs. If our current budget, and past financial reports also, did not show such an allocation for research, the clients and donors would have every right to say: "Put your money where your mouth is!"

The example above illustrates why budgeting is such a key step in the overall management process of non-profit charitable organizations. When we budget, we "put our money where our mouth is," or, in better words, we allocate our resources to fulfill our missions. If something we do is more important than other things we do, then our budgetary allocations should reflect this. When our words and our budgets are in tune, we can go to our clients, volunteers, and potential donors in full honesty. We can then appeal to them in a forthright manner: "Support us this year, and this is what we will do. Be involved with us this year, and you'll help us to take steps towards mission fulfillment." With appropriate budgeting, we'll find it easy to be a transparent organization, because we will have the confidence that we have full integrity.

The discussion on budgeting in this chapter will proceed as follows. I will start with a presentation of basic fundamentals of budgeting in non-profit organizations. Second, I will describe the various kinds of non-profit budgets. Then, I will recommend a specific budgeting process, composed of nine steps and aimed at involving the total organization. Fourth, I will present a budget format that I have seen to be effective. I will close the chapter with some comments on two important issues related to non-profit budgets, namely, financial reserves and balanced versus deficit budgets.

Fundamentals of Budgeting

When an organization approaches the budgeting process, where does it start? Does it look at its potential **income** first, or does it look at its projected **expense?** The idealistic way is to estimate expense first. In other words, those involved ask the question: "What do we need this next year to fulfill our mission?" Once this question is answered, then we proceed to determine the income necessary to support the expense need. On the other hand, the realistic approach deals with income first and asks the question: "How much money can we realistically raise next year?" Once this is determined, then we go on to adjust our projected expense and program plans to correspond to the projected income.

During my career, I've always wanted to approach the budgeting process in the idealistic way. I've even been a part of some real attempts at this, almost always in regard to other smaller non-profit organizations in which I happened to be involved. But, frankly, I've never seen it work. It always created a lot of excitement around the process, but, when it finally didn't work – in the sense that the budget was not actually achieved – the organizations ended up being frustrated, and even disillusioned, by the process. Thus, I believe that we have to settle for the realistic approach. We need first to make a realistic assessment of how much financial resource will be available to our organization next year, both through reserves and anticipated income, and then establish this as a control amount for projected program expense. This does not mean that we cannot try to stretch our income capability in response to the needs we perceive among our client population. But an organization cannot stretch too much, lest it create false expectation among clients and program staff and volunteers.

In some sense, this discussion about realistic and idealistic approaches to budgeting is quite theoretical. In the practical order, some people in non-profit organizations tend to be more realistic. These are the Treasurer, Staff Executive, Fundraising staff, and Budget Committee. Others tend to be more idealistic. These are the Program staff and Program Committee volunteers, who are very close to the clients. It is up to key people in the organization – most often the Staff Executive working with the Treasurer and Chair of the Board – to moderate any tension between these two factions, to balance the priorities between them, and to coordinate everyone with the goal of establishing a budget that all can live with.

Kinds of Budgets

The most common type of budget is called **operating.** This is the budget that usually contains most of the income and expense of an organization or those revenue and expenditure numbers intended to project and control the day-to-day functioning of the organization. Boards of Directors and staff leaders focus primarily on the operating budget as they lead the organization throughout the year.

But most organizations also have a **capital** budget. This projects and controls the financial numbers involved with property, equipment and other similar items. Included in the capital budget are those items of a pre-determined value (perhaps $500 or more) and which have a useful life of over one year. So, for example, the purchase of a computer for $1,200 would be in the capital budget, while the purchase in the same amount of stationery to be used throughout the year would be covered by the operating budget. Boards of Directors are asked to approve both operating and capital budgets with separate consideration given to each.

Some non-profit organizations also have **restricted** budgets. These involve the income and related expense of money given to the organization for a specific purpose by a donor or granting agency. Depending on the amount of funds so restricted and the wishes of the donor, an organization may decide to segregate the budgeting of these funds so that all concerned can project and monitor their use. But it is not essential that this be done, and restricted funds can be kept in the operating budget as long as the specific purpose of the restricted monies is part of the regular programming of the organization and their expenditure can be monitored appropriately through adequate financial reporting.

Finally, there are two kinds of operating budgets. One is **line item**, and the other is **program**. Line item budgets project and control income by source and expense by object. Such budgets list sources of income – for example, contributions, special events, and grants – and objects of expense – for example, salaries, rent, and postage – and project these for the coming year. On the other hand, program budgets, even though they also use line items, project and control income by the purpose for which it is received and expense by the purpose for which it is spent. In general, the larger an organization's budget is and the more distinct are its various activities, the more likely is the use of program budgeting. Likewise, the smaller the budget and the less distinct its activities, the more likely it is that the organization will use only line item budgeting.

Figure 2 illustrates this difference between line item and program budgeting, utilizing a total organization operating budget of $500,000:

Figure 2
Line Item and Program Budgeting

Line Item	TOTAL	Prog. A	Prog. B	Management	Fundraising
INCOME					
Contributions	200,000	25,000	25,000		150,000
Special Events	50,000	20,000			30,000
Grants	150,000		135,000	15,000	
Other Income*	100,000	20,000	20,000	10,000	50,000
Total Income	**500,000**	**65,000**	**180,000**	**25,000**	**230,000**
EXPENSE					
Salaries	300,000	100,000	120,000	40,000	40,000
Rent	35,000	12,000	15,000	3,000	5,000
Postage	15,000	6,000	3,000	1,000	5,000
Other Expense*	150,000	62,000	62,000	6,000	20,000
Total Expense	**500,000**	**180,000**	**200,000**	**50,000**	**70,000**

* The expressions "Other Income" and "Other Expense" above are used for purposes of simplification and ease of understanding. In a real budget presentation, several other kinds of income and expense would be listed. Examples of other income would be service fees, investment earnings, memberships, major gifts, and bequests. Examples of other expense would be employee benefits, payroll taxes, utility costs, telephone, travel, and professional fees.

The line item budget is seen in the first two columns. The sources of income and the objects of expense are listed in the first column, and the total amounts of each line item are in the second column. Four program budgets are seen in the next four columns. Note that the total amount of the four program budgets, taken together, equals the total amount of the line item budget.

The principle advantage of program budgeting is that it allows the staff executive to assign responsibility for each separate program to a different staff person or program head. In this way, accountability is distributed throughout the organization. The disadvantage of program budgeting is that it can diminish the overall influence of the staff executive, who may find it easier to track income by its various sources and to control expense by object. Overall accountability is very clear in an organization that uses line item budgeting. It lies solely with the staff executive. As stated before, however, the budget size and complexity of each organization usually determines the type of operating budget that is utilized, either line item or program.

Throughout my years with the Arthritis Foundation, we basically used a line item budget. Even though the dollar amounts were relatively large – up to 2.5 million – and we had five distinct programs (research, education, patient service, management, and fundraising), there was much overlap in expense from program to program, especially in regard to the major expense of staff salaries. As a result, we found it impractical to use program budgeting, but I tried hard to assign financial responsibility for the various program areas to different staff as far as it was possible.

For clarity of presentation in the remainder of this chapter, we will discuss budget development in an operating, line item sense. The principles are the same, whether they are about operating, capital, or restricted budgets, and a program budget is but a distinct part of an overall line item budget, as was made clear in Figure 2.

A Nine-Step Budgeting Process

Thinking about suggesting a process to be used in budgeting for a non-profit charitable organization reminds me of a saying often used by Bill Mulvihill of the University of Cincinnati and former National Chair of the Arthritis Foundation: "People support what they have had a part in deciding." This statement applies to many activities in an organization and generally in all of life, but I believe that it has particular importance to the development of an organization's budget where the support of everyone involved is critical not only to the budget development itself, but also to the successful implementation of that budget. Real ownership of the budget is essential throughout the organization, among all staff and volunteer leaders whose decision making on a day-to-day basis will influence the group's adherence to that budget. Any budgeting process must keep this goal of widespread ownership in sight as it proceeds ahead.

Another issue needs to be discussed before we move into the budgeting process. Who should lead this process? I feel strongly that the Staff Executive is in the best position to be the leader. He or she has – or should have – a comprehensive over-view of the financial situation of the organization that no one else has. There are certainly other key people in the process, especially the Treasurer of the Board, with whom the Staff Executive should work in partnership. But the leadership of the bud-geting process is one responsibility that the Staff Executive cannot delegate. That responsibility can be shared among other staff and volunteer leaders, but it cannot be delegated. When all is said and done, the Staff Executive is ultimately accountable for the budget's implementation.

There are certainly many different ways that the Staff Executive can lead a budget-ing process that will result in an appropriate operating budget that is truly owned by staff and volunteer leaders throughout the organization. But I suggest the following step-by-step process because it has worked for me and for others. (This presentation assumes a fiscal year beginning on January 1.)

Step 1 – Gathering Information: The summer months present a good time to start the process by gathering information, both formally and informally, on program and fundraising plans from staff and volunteer leaders. Program leaders can meet to de-velop their preliminary plans for the next year and then present these plans, together with their financial implications, to the Staff Executive. Fundraising staff and com-mittees can also to do something similar in regard to their development projections and plans. But informal and individual conversations with these same people and other significant leaders in the organization, especially the officers of the Board, can be just as important in this early phase of the budgeting process. I have found that the insights learned and honesty expressed in these informal ways often go far beyond what people are able to share in formal ways, and, as a result, they present truly useful information that cannot be gained in any other way. However this first step is accomplished, it is then the responsibility of the Staff Executive, perhaps with the assistance of the Staff Accountant, to summarize the information gathered into a comprehensive format that can be utilized in the subsequent steps.

Step 2 – Consideration of Salary Expense: Because salary expense usually rep-resents the highest percentage among all line items in the budget, this subject needs consideration early in the process. In my case, I benefited from a Salary Committee (oftentimes called a Personnel Committee), composed of a few key Board members, that convened next in the process. I was the only staff person to meet with this committee so that we could have a frank and open discussion. The agenda of this committee concentrated on the following matters:

1) the overall financial condition and performance of the organization;

2) general economic conditions affecting cost of living in our area;

3) current salary information gained from our national organization and local salary surveys;

4) a review of our organization's salaries now being paid; and

5) a discussion of current staff performance and the need for additional funds in the budget to reward exceptional performance of individual staff and/or to add new staff positions.

I was very active in this fifth agenda item, because it was my opportunity to be an advocate for staff members who were performing at high levels and to gain support for additional staff if and when I thought them to be necessary.

Following this far ranging discussion, the Salary Committee then made four basic decisions in regard to financial information for the next year's budget:

1) an amount of money needed to give all staff a cost of living raise;

2) an additional amount for merit raises for high performance staff;

3) funds for new staff if needed;

4) and, finally, and only after excusing me from the meeting room, an amount to cover my personal salary for the coming year.

I was then able to take this information and add it to the other material gained from step one. It is important to mention at this point that this proposed salary information was carried forward throughout the rest of the process as one number in order to protect the confidential matters discussed by the Salary Committee.

Step 3 – First Draft of the Budget: It was then time, usually in late September, for me to do a first draft of the budget. I found this to be an enjoyable and relatively easy task, especially in more recent times when spreadsheet technology is readily available. (I really love spreadsheets!) I wasn't very critical at this time, but essentially just put on paper the income and expense numbers I had gathered in steps one and two. The Staff Accountant could also develop this first draft with the guidance of the Executive.

Step 4 – Analysis of the First Budget Draft: Then it was time to make a full analysis of the first budget draft and to make the necessary adjustments. Invariably there is a huge gap between income and expense at this point. This results from the facts that the fundraising staff and volunteers have been conservative in their projections, while the program staff and volunteers have been expansive in their planning. Thus, the Staff Executive needs to go back to both groups to explain the reality of the situation and to seek their cooperation in increasing income on the one hand and decreasing expenses on the other. I never found this step to be an easy one. It took patience, understanding, and skills in persuasion. But it was an essential step, and I constantly reminded myself that "People support what they have a part in deciding."

Step 5 – Preparation of Preliminary Budget: Now the Staff Executive, perhaps with the assistance of the Staff Accountant, needs to prepare a preliminary budget that represents the thinking of everyone in the process, but that has been adjusted to reflect the reality of current organizational life and potential. This requires much judgment on the part of the Staff Executive at this point. And being able to consider many different "what if" possibilities, using spreadsheet technology, is a real asset to this critical step in the budgetary process. The product of this step should be a proposed budget that is achievable and reasonably balanced between income and expense. It should be a budget that the Staff Executive can truly live with and one that he or she is convinced will advance the mission of the organization at this particular time.

Step 6 – Involvement of the Board Treasurer: Now it is time to involve the Board Treasurer in a formal, definitive way. (However, the smart Staff Executive has been consulting with the Treasurer from time to time throughout the preceding steps.) The Board Treasurer needs to own the proposed budget to a greater degree than any other volunteer leader. He or she has the responsibility to carry it forward to Board approval and to report on the organization's financial performance in relation to budget as the year progresses. Therefore, the Staff Executive needs to spend as much time as is necessary to fully explain to the Treasurer the budget development steps that have already been taken and the reasons behind every item in the proposed budget. The Staff Executive must also be open to some modification in the proposed budget suggested by the Treasurer. It is only this openness that will convince the Treasurer that his or her Board responsibility is taken seriously and that he or she is truly "in charge" of the process from here on.

Step 7—Meeting of Budget or Finance Committee: Now, with staff assistance, the Treasurer convenes the organization's Budget or Finance Committee to fully discuss the proposed budget, modify it if need be, and to approve it before it is sent on to the Board of Directors for final approval. (Because we are drawing near to the end of the process, we are in late October or early November. There is a complete timeline of this budgeting process at the end of this section in this chapter.) Because of the critical importance of this step in the process, it is essential that all interests in the organization are adequately represented on the Budget Committee. In addition, I believe strongly that some of the same key volunteer and staff leaders, who participated in the early stages of budget development, should be on the Committee or at least invited to attend. Only such broad representation can guarantee a full airing of the proposed budget and its ramifications.

It is extremely important, in order to assure the effectiveness of this step in the process, that the members of the Budget Committee and all other attendees receive and review ahead of time the proposed budget and explanatory narrative. (The content of the "explanatory narrative" will be explained later on in this chapter.) This will enhance the quality of the discussion immeasurably.

The Treasurer, with the assistance of the Staff Executive, should lead the Budget Committee meeting. I usually found that, if I had done my work appropriately in the previous step, the Treasurer and I presented ourselves at the meeting as partners, as joint advocates of the proposed budget, and yet as open to changes that might come from the discussion. We spent a lot of time explaining to those in attendance the many compromises that had to be made, in both programming and fundraising, to arrive at the budget presented to the group. We also encouraged an open discussion, with disagreements freely being expressed. And, when a majority advocated changes in the budget, we accepted them. But, frankly, these changes were relatively few and quite minor, especially if we took real care and expertise in all the steps up to this point. The final action of the Budget Committee is to approve the proposed budget, as amended, and to pass it on to the Board of Directors with a recommendation for its final approval.

Step 8 – Final Approval of the Board: Now is the time for the last step in the budget development process, usually the November meeting of the Board of Directors. Just as with the Budget Committee, all Board members must receive the proposed budget and narrative well ahead of time to enable them to review them before the meeting. Approval of the annual budget must be seen as one of the most important Board decisions of the whole year.

The Treasurer presents and explains the proposed budget to the Board at the meeting, not only with the assistance of the Staff Executive, but now also with the support of the Budget Committee. My experience is that this part of the Board's agenda that day is dominated by explanation and response to questions and has very little disagreement, provided again that all previous steps have been done properly. The formal approval of the Board usually flows easily, especially considering that almost all Board members, one way or another, have "had a part in deciding" what was finally presented to them.

Another Possible Step -- Adjustments: Many organizations, including the Arthritis Foundation when I was its Staff Executive, have found it helpful to add another final step to the budget development process. This is to re-convene the Budget Committee in late January, after all of the actual financial report numbers have been finalized for the previous fiscal year, to review the situation with the benefit of this more complete financial picture and to determine if any adjustments need to be made in the approved budget for the year. If any adjustments are agreed upon at this meeting, they are then taken to the Board of Directors at its February meeting for approval, following the same procedures as before.

Budget Process Summary: Given the fact that I have described a lengthy and complex process over several pages, I will summarize it here with a suggested timeline and assuming a fiscal year that starts on January 1:

      Step 1 – July-August: Gathering Information

      Step 2 – Early September: Consideration of Salary Expense

      Step 3 – Mid September: First Draft of the Budget

      Step 4 – Late September: Analysis of the First Budget Draft

      Step 5 – Early October: Preparation of Preliminary Budget

Step 6 – Mid October: Involvement of the Board Treasurer

Step 7 – Late October: Meeting of the Budget or Finance Committee

Step 8 – November: Final Approval of the Board

Step 9 – Late January: Adjustments, if Needed

The Budget Format

There are many possible formats for the presentation of a budget. But I believe that there are four essential components of an effective presentation: 1) an introductory narrative, 2) an explanation of significant line items in the budget, 3) a statement of proposed income and expense with historical data, and 4) a month-by-month cash flow projection of the income and expense. Let's take a look at each one of these.

Introductory Narrative: When asking others – Treasurer, Budget Committee, other management staff, or Board of Directors – to review a proposed budget for the next year's income and expense, I always wanted them to understand the organizational context in which the budget was being presented. With this in mind, I would write about a one-page narrative containing explanations of such items as:

1) the status of the organization's financial reserves (Are they weak or strong?);

2) the current plans for programming and staffing (Are we expanding or contracting?);

3) the success of present and future fundraising efforts (Are fundraising results getting better or worse or staying the same?);

4) the proposed budget's relationship with the organization's strategic plan (Are there issues in the plan that must be considered along with the budget?);

5) capital expense needs (Are there major capital expenditures that need to be provided for?); and

6) other relevant information.

An introductory narrative such as this gives all reviewers a framework through which they can look at the numbers they are about to see and discuss. In sum, the narrative brings all reviewers up to speed with the overriding issues of the organization – those issues that are on the mind of the experienced Staff Executive all the time as he or she makes day-to-day administrative decisions and looks into the future.

Explanation of Line Items: In any numerical presentation of projected income and expense, there are many significant line items that need to be explained either because they are major in nature (salaries, for example), they are increasing or decreasing, they are new or different, or they are just not generally understood very well. Even though I usually would write this explanation after the numerical presentation was done, I found it helpful to include it ahead of the numerical information so that the reviewers would have a perspective on what they were about to see and also know what they could refer back to when they were not clear about the numbers they were reviewing. (I am sure that some could make an equal case for including this explanation after the numbers.) In general, when I wrote the line item explanation, I tried to anticipate questions that reviewers would have in looking at the numerical presentation.

Proposed Income and Expense: Now we come to principal part of the budget presentation, the projection of income and expense into the next year. The first point I wish to make here is that it is very important to present historical financial data before we actually get to the projected year. I found this to be helpful not only for those reviewing the proposed budget once it was drafted, but also helpful to the budget drafter (in this case, the Staff Executive) as it was being created. I illustrate this point in Figure 3, using again the $500,000 budget as seen in Figure 2.

As presented here, there are two years of audited (or actual) numbers before we even get to the current year (09) and proposed year (10). Then the current year's budget is followed by other actual numbers of the organization's financial performance for the first nine months of the year (09-9 Months) and an estimate of how the year will finish (09 Estimate). Only after this history is presented is the projection into the proposed year (10 Proposed) being made. This allows the reviewer, as his or her eyes move across the page, to see the proposed budget in the context of some history. For example, the reviewer can see that there has been a steady growth in total income over 3 years and that the income has kept relatively good pace with total expense. (The only apparent shortcoming is the $41,968 deficit

Figure 3
Historical Budget Presentation

Line Item	07 Audit	08 Audit	09 Budget	09-9 Months	09 Estimate	10 Proposed
INCOME						
Contributions	144,947	151,376	180,000	95,003	178,000	200,000
Special Events	34,101	41,472	45,000	36,422	47,000	50,000
Grants	135,000	140,000	150,000	120,000	150,000	150,000
Other Income	71,823	79,631	85,000	62,585	84,000	100,000
Total Income	385,871	412,679	460,000	315,010	459,000	500,000
EXPENSE						
Salaries	241,322	249,781	285,000	222,676	283,000	300,000
Rent	32,000	32,000	36,000	26,200	36,000	36,000
Postage	11,101	11,551	12,000	7,321	13,000	14,000
Other Expenses	109,234	117,962	127,000	101,781	130,000	150,000
Total Expense	393,657	411,294	460,000	356,978	462,000	500,000
Surplus (Deficit)	(7,786)	1,385	0	(41,968)	(3,000)	0

being run through 9 months in the current year. But this can be easily explained in the line item narrative by stating that the contributions, historically speaking, in the first income row have increased significantly in the last quarter of the year.) This will allow the reviewer to have real confidence in the organization's ability to budget accurately and to operate within the limits of the budget.

But this is not all that an historical presentation of a budget done in this manner illustrates. One can see other important details as well. For example, the reviewer can easily see what income categories are steadily growing (Contributions) and which ones are relatively static (Grants). The same is true for the expense line items. All of this enables the reviewer to understand that the proposed budget is consistent with the past and present. Or, if there is a real departure from the past and present in any category or overall, the difference will be clearly seen and explainable. The end result will be that, when reviewers, whether they be Budget Committee or Board members, are asked to approve the proposed budget, they will know exactly what they are being asked to approve, be able to ask appropriate questions and make reasonable suggestions for change, and, most importantly, be real owners of the budget once it is approved.

Month-by-Month Cash Flow Projection: It is one thing to develop a budget that shows income and expense for the total year. Also necessary is to illustrate how income and expense flows across the year on a month-by-month basis. I used to do this after the income and expense budget for the year was finally approved, but, because we had ample financial reserves, the budgeted cash flow was not a critical issue to the budget approval process. However, if an organization does not have ample reserves or if there are other important cash flow considerations (the timing of investment maturities, for example), it may be necessary to do the cash flow projection much earlier in the budget approval process.

Figure 4 gives an example of a month-by-month cash flow projection, using the same $500,000 budget. There are several items to point out in this cash flow projection, all of which will illustrate the importance of this budgeting exercise. First of all, it indicates that, in most non-profit charitable organizations, income tends to vary on a month-to-month basis, while expenses tend to be relatively consistent. Note that the "Total Income" ranges from $61,000 in January to the $10,000 in February. The projected "Total Expense" ranges from only $39,000 (January) to $44,000 (March and October). These differences can create some serious cash flow problems for the organization that does not anticipate them. For example, if you look at the "Surplus (Deficit)" and "YTD Balance" rows, you will see that the organization projects to have rather consistent deficits for the first eight months of the year, reaching an accumulative high of $57,000 in August. Only after that will the financial operation turn around and work back gradually towards the goal of being balanced. Thus, the organization can plan to have reserves ready to support the deficit operation for the larger portion of the year. Or, if lacking reserves, it can try to accelerate some income, delay some expense, or even get a short-term loan if there is no other alternative.

Figure 4
Month-by-Month Cash Flow Projection

Line Item	TOTAL	Jan	Feb	Mar	April	May	June	July	Aug	Sept	Oct	Nov	Dec
INCOME													
Contributions	200000	4000	2000	8000	12000	19000	15000	10000	10000	15000	20000	35000	50000
Special Events	50000				15000	10000					15000	10000	
Grants	150000	50000		30000			30000			40000			
Other Income	100000	7000	8000	9000	9000	10000	6000	5000	5000	10000	12000	12000	7000
Total Income	500000	61000	10000	47000	36000	39000	51000	15000	15000	65000	47000	57000	57000
EXPENSE													
Salaries	300000	25000	25000	25000	25000	25000	25000	25000	25000	25000	25000	25000	25000
Rent	36000	3000	3000	3000	3000	3000	3000	3000	3000	3000	3000	3000	3000
Postage	14000	1000	1000	1000	2000	1000	1000	1000	1000	1000	1000	2000	1000
Other Expense	150000	10000	11000	15000	12000	13000	12000	13000	12000	13000	15000	11000	13000
Total Expense	500000	39000	40000	44000	42000	42000	41000	42000	41000	42000	44000	41000	42000
Surplus(Deficit)	0	22000	-30000	3000	-6000	-3000	10000	-27000	-26000	23000	3000	16000	15000
YTD Balance		22000	-8000	-5000	-11000	-14000	-4000	-31000	-57000	-34000	-31000	-15000	0

37

It is important to note here that the cash flow problems exhibited in Figure 4 above are relatively mild compared to what often happens in the real world. My experience with the Arthritis Foundation reflected a much greater disparity between expected income and expense during the first several months of the year. For this reason, I wish to discuss here the importance of having a significant financial reserve.

Financial Reserve

I can remember early in my professional career that a non-profit charitable organization, which had a substantial financial reserve, was frequently looked upon with some derision by funding groups and individual donors. When they discovered the reserve position, their response might have been something like this: "You're doing fine. You don't need money from us." I'm pleased to report that this seems to be no longer the case. People now generally recognize that a non-profit organization, just like any business, needs a reserve to get it through the peaks and valleys of its financial life.

But how much of a reserve is appropriate? During my years with the Arthritis Foundation, there was a National policy for each Chapter to maintain a reserve equal to at least 50% (and not more than 100%) of the cost to operate for a year. I was grateful for this policy for three reasons. First, it enabled us to survive during those first several months of the year when the flow of income lagged considerably behind our required expense. Second, it gave everyone involved, especially the staff, a sense of security that we could meet current expenses even if income did not come in as expected. And, third, it enabled us to more easily explain to prospective donors the reasons why we maintained a reserve of this size. It was a National policy after all.

Some may question the need for a reserve of 50% to 100% of a projected annual operating cost. It is true that a financial reserve that appears to be too large is a turn off to prospective donors. But the Arthritis Foundation had legitimate, easily explainable reasons for such a reserve. We regularly made advance commitments for substantial research grants that spanned more than one year. But not all organizations make such commitments. So I return to the original question. What is an appropriate size of a financial reserve? Each organization needs to decide this for itself. But I strongly believe that any non-profit charitable organization needs and can justify a financial reserve of 25% of expected annual operating cost. Therefore, every budgeting process needs to consider the establishment and maintenance of an appropriate financial reserve for the organization.

Balanced and Deficit Budgets

A primary goal of the budget development process is clearly to end up with an approved budget that is relatively equal in proposed income and expense. One can rightly say that to plan to operate with a deficit budget – that is a plan to have more expense than income – is a plan to go out of business. But there are some instances when an apparent deficit budget may be quite strategic and appropriate. For example and provided that there are reserves to support it, a non-profit charitable organization may plan to stretch programmatically for a year or two in order to provide additional services based upon a conviction that this stretch will result in additional funding in the near future. Another example might be that an organization decides to spend down its reserves when these reserves are judged to be too great. (This was the case when Arthritis Foundation Chapters across the country found themselves in the rare and enviable position of having a reserve of more than 100% of projected annual operating cost.) In both examples, we are really not talking about a deficit budget, especially considering that the reserves used to support this apparent deficit are actually the result of income generating activities in previous years.

Bullet Summary

♦ Budgeting is a process by which a non-profit charitable organization plans to allocate its financial resources to fulfill its mission at a point in time.

♦ For many practical reasons, non-profit organizations usually consider potential income rather than expense first in the budgeting process.

♦ There are operating, capital, and restricted budgets, but non-profit organizations usually give the most focus to operating budgets.

♦ Non-profit organizations commonly use both line item and program budgeting, and each has its own advantages and disadvantages over the other.

♦ A successful, annual budgeting process usually takes about six months and ideally the Staff Executive leads the process.

♦ Realizing that people support what they have had a part in deciding, the competent Staff Executive will lead a budgeting process that is as democratic as possible, involving volunteer and staff leaders every step of the way, giving emphasis to the participation of the Treasurer and Budget Committee.

♦ There are four essential components of an effective budget format, namely, an introductory narrative, explanations of important line items, a presentation of past, current, and proposed income and expense, and a month-by-month cash flow projection.

♦ A successful non-profit organization needs to plan for and maintain an adequate financial reserve, at least equal to 25% of proposed annual operating expense.

♦ The goal of the budgeting process is to conclude to a budget approved by the Board of Directors that is relatively balanced between income and expense, with the income coming from either current revenue or a combination of current revenue and transfers from adequate reserves.

Conclusion

Budgeting is a democratic process resulting in an approved financial goal for the year that everyone in the organization supports. This leads to the next chapter on financial reporting, by which non-profit charitable organizations monitor their own progress in budget implementation and inform the public, donors, and other interested people about their current financial operation.

Suggested Readings

Brinckeroff, <u>Financial Empowerment: More Money for More Mission, an Essential Guide for Not-for-Profit Organizations</u>, John Wiley and Sons, New York, 1996, pp. 118-133.

Konrad and Novak, op.cit., pp. 27-42.

McLaughlin, op.cit., 129-143.

Chapter 4: **My Gut Tells Me It's Okay:**

Financial Reporting in Non-Profit Organizations

Several years ago, I was talking with a good friend, who was the dedicated staff executive of a relatively large non-profit charitable organization. She explained that the organization was struggling financially, that several Board members and staff were expressing concern to her, and that the financial reports – at least as far as she could understand them – indicated that there were some problems. Then she remarked: "My gut tells me it's okay." I worried about my friend after that conversation. In financial matters she shouldn't have been relying on her "gut." In her position, she should fully understand her organization's financial reports and every possible implication that may flow from them. No others in the organization – whether they are on the Board or staff – should have a greater understanding than she. I learned that she lost her job several months later. I was saddened to learn this, but, given the conversation we had, not at all surprised.

The story above illustrates clearly the extreme importance of a full understanding of the financial reports in non-profit charitable organizations, especially on the part of staff executives, Board members, and other management staff. I am not arguing that all these leaders need to be accountants, although an accountant or two on the Board of Directors is a great asset. But I do argue that leaders in these organizations need to know what they are seeing when they look at a financial report and fully understand the implications of the numbers contained there. Otherwise there is no way that they can carry out their fiduciary responsibility.

In my experience, too many Board members and staff leaders simply do not know what to look for when they review a financial report. They see a page or pages of numbers, are confused by them, and their eyes gloss over. Then they say something like this to themselves: "I'm just not a numbers person. But other people here are. I'll let them review the report and tell the rest of us if there are any problems." Thus, the financial accountability for the organization ends up in the hands of only a few. And, too often after this happens, the organization makes inappropriate financial decisions and gets into financial difficulty.

Therefore, I write this chapter with these "non-numbers people" in mind. I hope to give them enough financial acumen to enable them to carry out their fiduciary responsibility. My presentation follows this outline. First, I will define the two basic components of a non-profit organization's financial report. Then, I will look at the first component, the "Statement of Financial Position." Third, I will discuss the second component, the "Statement of Activities." Fourth, I will illustrate the point that different audiences need different kinds and frequencies of financial reports. Finally, I will mention and describe two financial reports, namely, the one done by an independent auditor and the IRS Form 990, both of which are essential for proper accountability to the public.

Components of a Financial Report

There are two basic components of a non-profit organization's financial report. The first is the "Statement of Activities" that lists the income and expenses over a certain period of time. (In the for-profit world, this is known simply as the "Income Statement.") The second component is the "Statement of Financial Position" that indicates the net worth of the organization at a certain point in time. (In the for-profit world, this is the "Balance Sheet.")

Let's consider first the "Statement of Activities." Notice that I have underlined above the phrase "over a certain period of time." Thus, this statement is an **active** one. It indicates the money that has come in (income) and the money that has gone out (expense) over a period in time, whether it is a month, a quarter, or a year. It concludes by indicating whether the organization, during the period of time, operated at a surplus (more income than expense) or at a deficit (more expense than income). On the other hand, the "Statement of Financial Position" is **static**, or, as underlined above, "at a certain point in time." It lists everything that the organization has (assets), both money and property, and then subtracts from that a list of everything owed by the organization (liabilities), and concludes to the net worth of the organization (net assets). So whatever point in time is at the top of the Statement of Financial Position, December 31 for example, the statement concludes that, if the organization had to close its doors on that day, it would be worth the amount listed as net assets.

From the discussion above, it is clear that there are just five basic accounts in the two components of an organization's financial report. These are income, expense, assets, liabilities, and net assets. Therefore, when someone is reviewing a financial report, he or she should look first for these five accounts. We will find these five accounts in a sample of a financial report later on, but let's see first how these five accounts interrelate by using three simple examples:

1. If an organization receives a $100 contribution, "income" is increased by $100, "assets" is increased by $100, and "net assets" is increased by $100.

2. If an organization pays a bill for $100, "expense" is increased by $100, "assets" is decreased by $100, and "net assets" is decreased by $100.

3. If an organization takes out a loan for $100, "income" is increased by $100 with the proceeds of the loan, "assets" is increased by $100, "liabilities" is increased by $100, and "net assets" remains unchanged.

I believe that, if a person knows where to find these five basic accounts and understands how the five accounts interrelate, he or she can review and understand any financial report no matter how complex that report may be.

Statement of Financial Position

In my experience, people have found it easier to understand the "Statement of Activities" than the "Statement of Financial Position." So let's take a closer look at this latter statement by comparing it to something more people might understand – the home mortgage:

Statement of Financial Position	Home Mortgage
Assets	Market Value
Liabilities	Loan Balance
Net Assets	Equity

With the home mortgage, the current "market value" less the "loan balance" equals the "equity" of the home. In like manner with the non-profit organization, the "assets" less the "liabilities" equals the "net assets" of the organization. Similarly, in the case of the home mortgage, there are two ways to increase the equity in the home, either by an increase in the market value or by a decrease in the loan balance.

Likewise there are two ways to increase the net assets of an organization, either by adding to some asset or by reducing some liability.

With the benefit of this general understanding, let's now look at a typical Statement of Financial Position of a non-profit organization:

Figure 5
Statement of Financial Position: 12/31/08 and 07

Assets:	2008	2007
CURRENT ASSETS		
Cash and Cash Equivalents	76,052	62,348
Contributions Receivable	20,000	15,000
Deposits and Pre-Paid Expenses	13,700	13,000
Total Current Assets	109,752	90,348
INVESTMENTS	98,765	84,674
PROPERTY AND EQUIPMENT, at cost		
Furniture and Equipment	43,731	41,894
Vehicles	18,921	20,223
Total Property and Equipment	62,652	62,117
Less Accumulated Depreciation	12,550	12,450
Property and Equipment, net	50,102	49,667
TOTAL ASSETS	**258,619**	**224,689**

Liabilities and Net Assets:

	2008	2007
LIABILITIES		
Accounts Payable	1,473	1,282
Accrued Expenses & Other Liabilities	22,345	20,886
Lease Obligations	14,000	28,000
TOTAL LIABILITIES	**37,818**	**50,168**
NET ASSETS		
Unrestricted	122,036	89,847
Temporarily Restricted	18,765	14,674
Permanently Restricted	80,000	70,000
TOTAL NET ASSETS	**220,801**	**174,521**
Total Liabilities and Net Assets	258,619	224,689

The Statement of Financial Position always compares the current year's (2008) position to the previous year's (2007) position. This allows the reviewer to see if the organization has grown in financial strength or not from one year to the next. Note that I have highlighted the numbers listed after three basic account titles in each column, namely, the numbers after "TOTAL ASSETS" (258,619 and 224,689), "TOTAL LIABILITIES" (37,818 and 50,168), and "TOTAL NET ASSETS (220,801 and 174,521). Thus, one can clearly see that, over the past 12 months, the organization increased its assets by about $34,000, decreased its liabilities by about $12,000, and, in sum, added to its net assets by about $56,000. Obviously, the organization has made significant gains in its financial strength. And the reviewer has made this important conclusion by looking only at the three basic accounts on this statement.

Note: Let's pause here to point out something that many find confusing in the Statement of Financial Position. The final line on the statement, "Total Liabilities and Net Assets," is often viewed at first as a significant number on the page, especially because of its placement at the end and because it is usually highlighted and underlined. But it is not a significant number at all, at least as far as an indication of financial strength. It is simply a balancing figure to show that the math on the page is accurate. In other words, the most significant number on the page is really the second to last line ("TOTAL NET ASSETS") and not the last line.

To continue on, once we look at the three basic accounts on the page and make some conclusion about the relative financial strength of the organization, then we can look at some other accounts on the page to see the details. For example, we can see that the primary asset increases are found in the available cash (almost $14,000) and in investments (about $14,000). In the same manner, we can see that the primary liability decrease has resulted in the reduction of lease obligations ($14,000). And, finally, we can see that the primary net asset gain has been in the unrestricted category (about $32,000). This is all important information, but it only serves to support the primary conclusion that the reviewer has already made by looking at the three basic accounts on the statement.

Statement of Activities

Let's now employ the same methodology as we review a typical Statement of Activities of a non-profit charitable organization, using the simplified format and the same numbers from the discussion on budget preparation in the previous chapter:

Figure 6
Statement of Activities: 9/30/08

Line Item	Total Budget for Year	Current Month			Year-to-Date		
		Budget	Actual	Variance	Budget	Actual	Variance
INCOME							
Contributions	200,000	15,000	16,746	1,746	95,000	99,812	4,812
Special Events	50,000			0	25,000	27,654	2,654
Grants	150,000	40,000	40,000	0	150,000	150,000	0
Other Income	100,000	10,000	9,075	-925	69,000	71,237	2,237
Total Income	**500,000**	**65,000**	**65,821**	**821**	**339,000**	**348,703**	**9,703**
EXPENSE							
Salaries	300,000	25,000	26,021	1,021	225,000	223,875	-1,125
Rent	36,000	3,000	3,000	0	27,000	27,000	0
Postage	14,000	1,000	1,134	134	10,000	10,762	762
Other Expense	150,000	13,000	14,322	1,322	111,000	109,445	-1,555
Total Expense	**500,000**	**42,000**	**44,477**	**2,477**	**373,000**	**371,082**	**-1,918**
Surplus (Deficit)	0	23,000	21,344	-1,656	-34,000	-22,379	11,621

In this typical statement dated 9/30/08, the intent is to inform the reviewer not only about financial activities during the month of September and the first nine months of the year, but also to illustrate how the organization is performing financially in relation to its budget. And just as we concluded from interpreting the Statement of Financial Position above, we can learn the important message of the statement by simply looking at the basic accounts, namely, in this case, income and expense. I have highlighted the numbers listed after "Total Income" and "Total Expense" all across the page. In the income row, we are first reminded about the total budget for the year of $500,000, and then this is broken down, according to the cash flow projection made in the beginning of the year, for the month of September (Current Month) to $65,000. Moving further from left to right in the same row, we see that the organization actually brought in $65,821, which is $821 over the projected budget. Moving further to the right, we view the same information for nine months of the year (Year-to-Date), that is, $339,000 in budget and $348,703 in actual achievement, for a positive variance of $9,703. Thus, by looking only at the one account of income, we can conclude that the organization has done well in comparison to its budget in both September and for nine months of the year. Then, if we would like to see more detail about this achievement, we can let our eyes go up the page to the other accounts to determine the specific reasons for the success. In doing this, we will easily conclude that the income "star" is "Contributions," which is responsible for more than all of the positive variance in September and for about half of the success for nine months.

Now let's view the account of expense in the same way. In the "Total Expense" row, we see first the $500,000 annual budget for the year, followed by the $42,000 monthly budget and the $44,477 actual expense in September, for an over-expenditure of $2,477. Then, looking at the year-to-date numbers, we see the $373,000 budget and the $371,082 actual expense, for an under-expenditure of $1,918. So, we can conclude quickly that the organization, although it exceeded its September expense budget, is doing well for the first nine months of the year in managing its expenses. And, in looking up the page at the various sub-accounts, we can learn about the specific reasons for this financial achievement.

Finally, after viewing the income and expense rows in the report and looking up the page for the details, we look at the "Surplus (Deficit)" row to see the bottom line conclusion of the presentation. Here the income and expense information is combined into net figures. As we move across the page from left to right, we see first that the budgeted goal for the whole year is to be in balance. Then we see that the budgeted goal for September was to have income exceed expense by $23,000. And excess of $21,344 was actually achieved, for a negative variance of $1,656. But, year-to-date, the organization is in very good shape, as the projected deficit for nine months of $34,000 is actually only $22,379, for a positive net variance of $11,621.

An actual Statement of Activities may be much more complex than this. It will always have more line item sub-accounts, as "Other Income" and "Other Expense" will be further delineated with what these really represent. (This was noted in the last chapter.) And there may be other columns that compare this year's achievements with those of the previous year. But, if our focus remains on the basic accounts of income and expense, at least as we first look at the statement, the detail will not confuse and frustrate us, and we will be able to understand what is really going on financially in the organization.

Differences in Kind and Frequency of Financial Reports
for Different Audiences

Although all financial reports contain the five basic accounts of income, expense, assets, liabilities, and net assets, there are many different kinds and they may cover different time periods, all determined by the different audiences for which they are intended. Let's look at these now as they relate to the various audiences.

Executive and Management Staff: As they oversee the day-to-day operation of the non-profit charitable organization, the executive and management staff need the frequent financial reports and oftentimes these can be very informal in nature. For example, during my years as a Staff Executive, I wanted to see financial information everyday. (That is why I was most comfortable when the office of the Staff Accountant was right next to mine!) I wanted to know how much income came in (and from whom), how much expense went out (and to whom), and how much money was in our operating account as a result. In this way, I kept abreast of our financial successes and failures on a daily basis and was not surprised at the end of a week or month to learn that we were in trouble or in a good place. I may have been overly conscientious in this matter (Our staff accountants over the years would probably agree!), but this was the only way I knew how to carry out my executive responsibility. And I strongly recommend that all staff executives be similarly conscientious, at least to some degree.

Other management staff persons need frequent financial reports, too, especially if they are responsible for departmental budgets and goals. For example, I was always encouraged and pleased when our Director of Development was more on top of the financial progress of a fundraising activity than I was, even if he or she was doing this with some informal set of financial tracking methods. I felt the same about our Program Director when he or she was fully aware of the approved expense levels for each program activity and managed to stay within those financial limits. In both cases, my anxiety stayed at a low level as we moved through the year, and I was able to lead the total operation of the organization with confidence, resulting from the knowledge that I was not alone in trying to be accountable for the financial resources entrusted to us.

Before ending this discussion about staff and financial reports, I want to mention the important role that other non-management staff can play. I was always greatly encouraged when other staff would take an interest in the financial matters of the organization and would perceive their respective responsibilities in regard to them.

One particular example of this is still very much in my memory. We were in a financial pinch, largely caused by a downturn in our fundraising success at the time. Before taking the drastic measure of laying off some staff, I decided to fully present the problems we were facing to all staff at a meeting. I asked all staff to come up with ideas for cutting costs. What a response they gave! All of a sudden we were receiving lower bids for printing and projects, and other new ideas for saving money were being presented to me almost everyday. As a result, we got through the crisis without having to cut back on staff, and, even when our fundraising success was restored, we carried forward many cost saving practices discovered through the process. I learned then – and never will forget – the immense value of involving all staff in the decisions that affect their employment lives, not only for their well-being, but also for the achievement of the mission of the organization.

Board of Directors: As was discussed in Chapter 2, non-profit Boards of Directors have the ultimate fiduciary responsibility for the finances of non-profit charitable organizations. They need to review and understand frequent, accurate, and comprehensive financial reports to carry out this responsibility. Therefore, the Board needs to be provided regularly with a Statement of Financial Position and a Statement of Activities, comparing current and year-to-date financial performance with both budget and the previous year.

How often should the Board review these financial statements? I believe strongly that a review needs to take place every month. If the Board does not meet monthly, then a Finance or Executive Committee can perform this important review function on the months that the full Board doesn't meet. Such frequency allows the Board of Directors to be made aware of financial problems long before they reach crisis stages and in plenty of time to take corrective action. I always welcomed this monthly review. It reminded all leaders in the organization, both volunteers and staff, of our responsibility to constantly operate within the boundaries of the approved budget and to work hard towards our fundraising goals. Thus, I was not alone in these concerns.

Finally, how should the Board review be accomplished? Clearly, the Treasurer of the Board has the responsibility to present the monthly financial report. But the Staff Executive – or another staff officer – has the duty to make it possible for the Treasurer to carry out this important task. In my case, shortly after I received and reviewed the monthly financial report from the Staff Accountant, I would prepare some explanatory notes for the Treasurer to use for his or her report to the Board. These notes would be about significant successes or failures in various income and expense accounts, giving explanations for the respective financial performance. I tried to anticipate the questions that Board members might have when they reviewed the report. Then I would share the report and my notes with the Treasurer, either in person or electronically. Then the Treasurer could add some personal thoughts to the notes, ask me any additional questions that he or she might have, and in this way be prepared to present the financial report to the Board at its meeting. I always considered it to be a failure on my part if the Treasurer was unable to respond adequately to any question or concern of a Board member expressed at the meeting.

Donors, Clients, and other Interested People: The primary way in which a non-profit charitable organization presents a financial report to its donors, clients, and other interested people is through the publication and distribution of an Annual Report. This report usually contains a summary of program activity for the year, a listing of the Board members and staff involved, and a full financial report. The Annual Report can be a relatively simple document produced in-house or an elaborate one produced by an outside printing company, containing more information and photos. In either case, the basic information listed above needs to be included in the report, and it needs to be distributed as widely as possible.

I have always found the Annual Report to be a very handy document to have around during the year. As we introduced new people to the organization, received donations from new donors, made requests for support to individuals and groups, or when people inquired about our programs or finances, we could give them a report as a basic introduction to our organization. Without a doubt, this enhanced our transparency in financial matters with people outside of our organization as we moved through the year. For these reasons, we always printed many more Annual Reports than were needed for the original distribution.

Independent Audit

Non-profit charitable organizations, with annual budgets of $500,000 or more, are required by law to have their financial records audited by an independent certified public accountant (CPA) upon the close of their fiscal year. In the practical order, however, almost all such organizations, no matter what their budget size, have an independent audit each year because it is required by many of their donors and granting institutions.

To fulfill this obligation, most non-profit charitable organizations actually hire a

CPA firm to perform the audit. However, it is permissible for an individual CPA or CPA firm to perform this service on a "pro bono" or reduced fee basis, as long as there is no evidence of conflict of interest.

The independent auditor reviews the financial transactions during the year to verify that the Staff Accountant has recorded them properly and that there is adequate documentation for them on file. In other words, the auditor does enough investigative work to ascertain with some level of confidence that the organization has spent its resources for the reasons it says it has, has recorded all support for the organization accurately, and has carried out the expressed intentions of any donors and granting institutions. Following this thorough investigation, the auditor issues a formal report to the Board of Directors indicating that the organization has – or has not – been accurate in its financial reporting and that these reports have been done in accordance with "generally accepted accounting procedures (GAAP)."

An Arthritis Foundation Board member, knowledgeable about legal matters, pointed out the importance of the independent audit to me once by stating emphatically that a Board of Directors should never be asked to formally **approve** a financial statement, unless that statement has been audited. So, as we moved through the year, the Treasurer would ask the Board to simply **accept** the monthly financial report. Only at year-end, when the Treasurer at the Annual Meeting presented a financial report that was based upon the independent audit, was the Board asked to formally **approve** it. This protected the Board from the legal liability that could result from its approval of a financial report prepared inappropriately or inaccurately by the organization's accounting staff.

The independent auditing firm performs another valuable service. It issues a "Management Letter" to the organization's Board and its management, which contains recommendations for improvement in financial record keeping, controls over money coming in and going out, and other accounting procedures. The letter makes it clear that the shortcomings discovered in these regards have not affected the accuracy of the organization's financial reports, but that the recommendations are only intended to bring about improvements in management operations. I have always found these annual letters to be very helpful to me in carrying out my executive responsibilities.

There is one final observation to make about the service of independent auditors. I have always found it useful to establish a personal relationship with them. This was relatively easy for me to do, especially because I grew to have a great deal of respect for them and their profession, and they frequently expressed a real interest in our mission and overall operation. And, once this relationship was established, I would seek their advice about organizational financial matters informally, both during their audits and other times during the year. These informal discussions oftentimes covered subjects beyond the audit or even the management letter, and we never were actually charged for such consultation. Rather the auditors considered this to be part of their service.

IRS Form 990

There is a final financial report of a non-profit charitable organization to be knowledgeable about. It is IRS Form 990, or the annual "tax return" of non-profit organizations. Even though 501(c)(3) organizations do not pay taxes, unless they have unrelated business income, which will be discussed in Chapter 6, they still have to file an annual tax return just like any business. This is a very extensive form, due each year 4 and 1/2 months after the close of the fiscal year, and the usual practice is to have the auditing firm prepare it for an additional fee. (However, some small organizations with little complexity may be able to complete the Form 990 themselves.) Some of the items of information required by the Form are as follows:

- Income, Expense, Assets, Liabilities, and Net Assets

- Program, Management, and Fundraising Expenses

- Amount of funds spent on lobbying

- A listing of Executive and higher level salaries

- A listing of donors and granting institutions contributing more than $5,000

Other basic information is required, but these are the most significant.

What is interesting and important about the Form 990 is that it has become the primary document for the public accountability of non-profit organizations. Besides filing it with the IRS every year, organizations must by law provide the completed form to anyone who asks for it. (Organizations can eliminate the information on the $5,000 plus donors before they provide the form in this instance.) I must admit that

I have never been overwhelmed with requests for our Form 990, but its importance and use seems to be growing every year. Many funding institutions ask for it before they will consider making grants. And I have seen that private entrepreneurs, as a service to major donors, have collected the Form 990's from many non-profit organizations to be able to share the information with the interested donors. As a result, it is becoming more and more common for non-profit charitable organizations to actually provide access to their completed Form 990 through their website. This is a good idea. It certainly indicates a willingness to be transparent in financial matters.

Bullet Summary

♦ Board members, staff executives, and other management staff need to fully understand financial reports if they are to carry out their fiduciary responsibilities.

♦ There are two major components of an organization's financial report, namely, the Statement of Activities and the Statement of Financial Position.

♦ These two statements contain five basic accounts (income, expense, assets, liabilities, and net assets), and these accounts are all inter-related.

♦ The Statement of Financial Position indicates the net worth of an organization **as of a certain date.** The Statement of Activities indicates an organization's income and expense **over a certain period of time.**

♦ There are differences in the kinds and frequency of financial reports depending on their intended audiences, whether they are executive, management, and other staff, the Board of Directors, and donors, clients, and other interested people.

♦ Most non-profit charitable organizations are required to have an independent audit upon the close of their fiscal year. The auditor's report is issued to the Board of Directors and notifies the Board that the organization's financial records are kept – or are not kept – in accordance with generally accepted accounting procedures.

♦ Even though non-profit charitable organizations usually do not pay any taxes, they are required by law to file an annual tax return, which is the Form 990. The completed Form must be shared with any member of the public that asks to see it.

Conclusion

Non-profit charitable organizations regularly report on their financial affairs to various audiences, ranging from their Boards of Directors to the general public. This is the primary way in which these organizations demonstrate accountability and transparency in their financial operation and indicate their seriousness in carrying out their fiduciary responsibility. This leads to the next chapter in which we describe the financial controls that are necessary for an organization to protect the assets that have been entrusted to it.

Suggested Readings

Brinckerhoff, op. cit., Financial Empowerment....., pp. 91-102.

Konrad and Novak, op. cit., pp. 43-58.

McLaughlin, op.cit., pp. 35-66.

Chapter 5: She Has Ruined My Business:

Controlling Financial Operations in Non-Profit Organizations

Early in my professional career, I wondered why there was such a high level of concern about internal controls in non-profit charitable organizations, especially considering that most of our financial transactions were by way of checks. I learned why one day in a very graphic way. A friend owned and operated a small copier paper supply business. Let's call it "Joe's Copier Paper Company." He was also the sales and delivery person. He had only one employee – a woman who staffed his office, took care of his simple financial records, opened the mail, paid the bills, and made bank deposits. As my friend was delivering a supply of copier paper to our office one day, I could see that he was quite distraught. When I asked him why, he said something like this: "I've only had one employee for the seven years of my business. She has run my office all these years and I have trusted her completely. I just found out yesterday that she's been stealing from me regularly – so much so that now she has ruined my business!"

When I asked my friend how she accomplished this, he explained that years ago, unknown to him, she had opened a second account in another bank in the name of "Joe's Copier Paper Company." She listed herself as the lone signer on the account. Then, as she opened the mail every day, she would siphon off a payment check or two once in a while and deposit them in the second account. Then, of course, from time to time she would issue a check to herself from this second account. Because she also kept the financial records and received almost no appropriate supervision, she was successful for many years in hiding the embezzlement from the owner. The end result was a theft of several thousand dollars that caused my friend to go out of business, not only because of the resulting financial stress, but also because of discouragement.

This real life story illustrates clearly how any business can be negatively affected if adequate financial controls are not in place. Such occurrences can and do happen in the non-profit charitable world, too, as much as we would like to say that they cannot and do not. And, because we are handling money "that is not our own" and people's lives are affected when we allow such things to happen, we must be even more vigilant.

This chapter will address the subject matter of financial controls in three parts. First, we will consider the essential role of the Staff Executive. Then, we will discuss the important oversight role of the Board of Directors. Finally, I will outline the actual rules and procedures that need to be in place.

Role of the Staff Executive

I was introduced to this topic back in 1976 when I was first hired to be the Chapter Executive in the Arthritis Foundation. I went to the National Office of the Foundation in New York City to receive some orientation to my responsibilities along with a few other new Chapter Executives. Early on in the program, the Senior Vice President of the National Office asked this question: "What is your most important responsibility as an executive?" We answered with responses like: "strategic planning," "raising lots of dollars," and "being faithful to the mission." The Senior Vice President then stated that, even though a good case could be made for each of our responses, he believed that the most appropriate answer is to "protect the assets of the organization." He went on to explain that we would probably not be forgiven by our Boards of Directors and would be placing our jobs in jeopardy if we failed in this major responsibility. To this day I still agree with his opinion.

As we discuss protecting the assets of a non-profit charitable organization, we need to realize that these assets are many. Some are human (staff, volunteers, clients, and donors); some are material (property and equipment); some are legal (501(c)(3) status and other exemptions); and some are financial (cash and investments). The Staff Executive needs to protect all of these, and one can make a case for the supreme importance of each. But we are talking about financial assets in this book. And, in my opinion, the Staff Executive is the pivotal person in the organization to assure that these assets are protected. In a word, to borrow a phrase from former President Harry Truman, "the buck stops here."

The Staff Executive needs to set a tone throughout the organization, both among staff and volunteers, that handling financial assets properly is important, that rules and procedures need to be followed, and that there is adequate oversight in place to keep everyone careful and honest. He or she is the primary "enforcer" of the financial control rules and lets it be known that any carelessness will simply not be tolerated. In addition, the Staff Executive needs to insist that all others in management positions appropriately enforce these same rules. My experience gives testimony that, if the Staff Executive assumes this leadership role in this way, then a concern about protecting financial assets does, indeed, permeate the total organization and become part of its culture.

The same applies to budget adherence, another way that organizations protect their financial assets. As discussed in Chapter 3, by approving a budget, the Board of Directors carries out its important responsibility to allocate the organization's financial assets to carry out the mission of the organization for a certain period of time. Then it becomes the responsibility of the Staff Executive to operate the organization in accordance with the approved budget. If he or she has a lackadaisical attitude about budget adherence and does not exercise real leadership in this regard, then there will be a poor attitude about budget adherence throughout the organization. On the contrary, if he or she demonstrates a true interest in the matters of the budget and insists that all live within its limitations, then a realization of the importance of budget adherence will permeate the organization and be part of its culture as well.

Role of the Board of Directors

Given the fact that the Board of Directors has the ultimate fiduciary responsibility for the financial affairs of the non-profit charitable organization, and even though the role of the Staff Executive is pivotal in the implementation of financial controls, the Board needs to exercise a significant oversight role in this regard. It performs this oversight role in three ways: through its Treasurer, at its Board meetings, and through its Committees.

Responsibilities of the Treasurer: The Board of Directors elects its Treasurer and defines the duties of this position according to the organization's By-Laws, which usually summarize the Treasurer's responsibilities something like this:

- To be the principal financial officer of the corporation;

- To hold, deposit, and maintain the safety of all financial assets of the corporation;

- To develop an annual budget for Board approval; and

- To make sure that the organization operates within the approved budget.

In the practical order, the Treasurer usually delegates the actual implementation of these responsibilities to the Staff Executive, Staff Accountant, or other senior management staff. But he or she must make the effort to know what is going on in all of these areas and to perform a genuine oversight role. And the Staff Executive must insist, with other staff and with the Treasurer himself or herself, that the Treasurer is to be involved in the decision making around financial matters, especially in regard to major issues like bank selection, investments, and budget variances. There is one responsibility, however, that the Treasurer should not delegate to staff. This is the responsibility of presenting and reviewing financial matters for the Board of Directors. He or she can rely upon – and should expect – assistance from staff in preparing to give financial reports to the Board, but the Treasurer needs to be the visible leader of financial matters in relation to the Board. Staff, of course, can speak on financial issues at Board meetings, but only upon the request of the Treasurer.

Responsibilities at Board Meetings: At the regular meetings of the Board of Directors, a major agenda item should be a full presentation of a current financial report done by the Treasurer. Included in this presentation should be explanations of all significant budget variances – both positive and negative – and discussion about financial trends in both income and expense as the organization moves through the year. The Treasurer should encourage questions from Board members on the financial report and respond to them as thoroughly as possible. (As a side note, I always considered it to be a personal failure if the Treasurer was unable to respond to a particular question, because this oftentimes meant that I had not done a good enough job in preparing him or her.) Sensitivity to such questions is an excellent way to reinforce the fact that the Board of Directors has the ultimate fiduciary responsibility for the financial affairs of the organization.

In addition to a monthly financial report, there are other financial matters that are to be brought to the Board of Directors for its approval or action. These include:

- Resolutions for all new or changed bank and investment accounts;

- Resolutions for Board member and staff signers on accounts;

- Approval of the organization's annual budget;

- Authorizations to exceed budgetary limitations;

- Approval of leases and other long-term financial commitments; and

- Review and approval of independent auditors' reports and recommendations.

Care should be taken to not let the Board conduct these financial actions in a perfunctory way. The best way to assure this is for the Treasurer, with the support of the Chair of the Board, to remind the members of the Board that, when they take such actions, they are making important decisions through which they are being accountable to donors, clients, and the public for the financial assets of the organization.

Responsibilities of Board Committees: The Board of Directors can effectively carry out its responsibilities for the financial matters of the non-profit charitable organization through the appointment of some key committees and clearly defining their respective roles. Such committees need to function in the areas of budget and finance, personnel, audit, and investments. Although, especially in smaller organizations, these functions may be combined into fewer committees, we will now summarize the functions of each.

The responsibilities of the **Budget and Finance Committee** include:

- Preparation of the annual budget for Board approval;

- Monitoring the organization's financial performance against budget, especially in those months when the Board does not meet; and

- Making recommendations to the Board on bank accounts and related matters.

The responsibilities of the **Personnel Committee** include:

- Discuss and establish an amount for salaries, including that of the Staff Executive, to be included in the annual budget for approval by the Board;

- Develop recommendations on bonuses and other staff incentive programs;

- Review staff benefits, especially retirement programs, and make recommendations on them; and

- Develop and review staff personnel policies.

The responsibilities of the **Audit Committee** include:

- Select the annual independent auditor for the organization and reach agreement with that auditor on the fee to be paid;

- Once the audit is completed, meet with the auditor and senior staff to discuss a draft of the audit report; and

Note: An important part of this annual meeting with the auditors during my career was that the Audit Committee would meet separately with the representatives of the auditing firm (that is without staff) for a few minutes after the general meeting to see if there were any problems working with our accounting staff and then, in turn, would meet separately with the senior staff to share any problems and to see if there were any problems working with the auditing firm. I always found this to be a valuable process to go through.

- Present the auditor's report, perhaps together with the auditor, to the Board of Directors.

The responsibilities of the **Investment Committee** include:

- Establish investment policies for the organization to make sure that investments align with – or at least do not contradict – the mission of the organization and are conservative in nature so that the financial assets are not put at risk;

- Make investment decisions, when the organization has the opportunity to do so because of the status of its financial reserves, in accordance with those policies; and

- Make selling decisions when funds are needed for the programs of the organization.

In concluding this section on the responsibilities of these financial committees, it must be clear from the outset that the committees function in a subsidiary role to the Board of Directors. Even if, as it is in some cases, these committees actually have the delegated authority to make final decisions (for example, the Investment Committee in making actual investment decisions or the Audit Committee in selecting the auditor), the Board cannot relinquish its oversight role in these matters, because it is in just such matters that the Board is most vulnerable to failure in carrying out its fiduciary responsibility.

Rules and Procedures for Financial Control

Throughout my career, I have come upon many rules and procedures that have been helpful to me in maintaining control over financial matters as a Staff Executive. I have learned some from auditors and other executives. Others I have found in my professional reading. Others are simply ideas that have worked for me. But nowhere have I seen a complete list of such rules and procedures. So that is what I will try to do here.

1. No one person should be allowed to handle all aspects of a financial transaction. My friend in the copier paper business made his mistake by not establishing and maintaining this rule. I grant that it may be a hard one to implement in a small company like his, but it always can be followed in some way. Some people refer to this as the "separation of duties." But, in any event, it is a key rule in financial control. It is based upon the conviction that it is harder for two people to agree upon a dishonest act than for one person to be dishonest.

How we implemented this rule with income transactions in our Chapter of the Arthritis Foundation went something like this. We received most of our income from the mail everyday. There may have been from 10 to 100 donation envelopes to open every day. Certain people, who had no other responsibility for financial matters, had the assignment each day to open the mail and to make a simple list of the of the donors, their contributions, and the total of these. (I would take on this duty on an assigned day to demonstrate that it was an important responsibility. And, if I had the opportunity to do it all over again, I would require that the assigned person do this in a common area of the office rather than in his or her private office.) Then the opened mail and checks were passed on to the person in charge of entering the donor information into our database. If that person did not conclude to the same number and amount of donations of the person before, then we knew that we had a problem to reconcile – and we did it then and there. Unfortunately, a third step was then required because the database did not interface with our accounting system. So the opened mail and checks were passed on to the Staff Accountant, who then entered the gross amounts into the accounting system and prepared the bank deposit. If he or she did not conclude to an identical amount of donations, then again we knew we had a problem to reconcile then and there. Thus, the original numbers, posted in a simple way by the person who opened the mail in the first place, became the control numbers for the whole process. I believe that this daily process not only reduced the likelihood of dishonesty, but also increased the level of accuracy in our whole system.

There certainly are a number of other ways to achieve the same level of separation in duties as money comes into the organization. The important point is to institutional-ize some process that achieves the same objectives.

Now let's look at how to provide the same level of safety on the expense side, where also the same person should not handle all aspects of the transaction. This is a much easier to implement by simply establishing a procedure whereby the person who prepares the checks is not permitted to sign them. So, in our case, the Staff Accountant would prepare the checks, attach the bill or invoice to each, and pass the checks on to the persons authorized to sign on the account. This is clearly an adequate separation of duties.

2. All financial transactions must have adequate documentation: First, in rela-tion to income transactions, implementing this rule means keeping and filing the letters, forms, envelopes, or other documentation that accompanies all donations and other income checks together with copies of the checks themselves or receipts. On the expense side, implementing this rule means attaching the bills and invoices to the disbursement checks until they are signed and sent and then filing them with copies of the checks afterwards. The Staff Executive must insist that all authorized signers on accounts not sign disbursement checks unless they have verified that there is adequate documentation and that the checks are issued to the appropriate payees and in the right amounts.

I have experienced only two difficulties in this regard. The first relates to Board members who are authorized signers. Oftentimes, when I would take checks to them for signature, and they would see that my signature was already on them, they might say something like this: "Since you have already signed them, I know that they must be okay. So I will just go ahead and sign them without looking at the documentation." I would always respond by insisting that they verify the documentation nonetheless. And, if they didn't have the time to do so, I would state that I would take them to someone else. In my opinion, this is an important accountability issue that should never be compromised.

I feel the same way about the other difficulty that has happened from time to time. This is when someone – usually a staff person – argues that a blank check needs to be signed. The typical circumstance is that a delivery is expected for which the amount of the bill is not known, the vendor requires immediate payment, and an authorized signer may not be available at the time. Whenever I was faced with such a request from staff or anyone else, I would simply respond that no check can be issued and signed without adequate documentation, and, if a vendor cannot accept this policy, we should choose another vendor. Frankly, I cannot imagine a circumstance that would justify a violation of this rule.

3. There should be two signatures on all disbursement checks, and one of these should be of a Board member: Unlike rules 1 and 2, this one is not generally accepted in the non-profit world. But I recommend it nonetheless, because it enhances accountability in a non-profit charitable organization in a very significant way. It enables the Board of Directors, through an authorized representative, to oversee every expenditure of funds entrusted to its care.

But why is this rule not generally accepted? I believe it is only an issue of convenience. In other words, some organizations argue that it is inconvenient to have a Board member countersign every check. In fairness to these organizations, I am not trying to say that they are entirely abandoning accountability, because they usually require a second signature by a Board member on all checks over a certain amount, for example, $200 or $500. But I do say that they are missing an opportunity to increase the accountability of their financial operations over an issue that can be easily resolved in other ways.

In my experience, we addressed the issue of inconvenience in the observance of this rule in two ways. First, I asked the Board to authorize some of its members to be signers on our accounts for reasons other than their office. In other words, besides authorizing the Chair and Treasurer to carry out this function, I asked that others be authorized who worked nearby or who for other reasons were easily accessible to perform this responsibility. Second, our normal routine was to process checks only twice per month. Thus, the necessity to seek out a second signature on disbursement checks was far from a daily or even weekly occurrence.

But how about the first signature on the checks? The usual and recommended practice is to have the Board of Directors authorize the Staff Executive to carry out this function. In his or her absence, another senior staff person – other than the Staff Accountant, of course – can be authorized to serve in this capacity. But in no instance should disbursements be implemented with only the signatures of two staff members. One signature of a Board member should always be required.

4. All financial operations and transactions should have regular and appropriate oversight: This rule is general in nature and covers a lot of territory. Its intent is to make sure that everyone who handles financial assets actually feels that he or she is not functioning in a vacuum or that someone else is aware of what is going on. I believe that examples are the only way to explain this rule.

A primary example is for the Staff Executive to regularly check the work of the Staff Accountant. I would do this by reviewing and signing off on the bank reconciliation done by the Staff Accountant each month. In the process, I would leaf through the cancelled checks to make sure that all were appropriately signed and that there were no unauthorized disbursements. Sometimes, too, I would intercept and review the monthly bank statement **before** the Staff Accountant had access to it.

Another good example is that supervisors review and approve all expense accounts before they are reimbursed. The Staff Executive needs to lead the way in this effort by submitting his or her expense accounts to the Board Chair or Treasurer before reimbursement. And all others should follow this lead. This is an important area to assure accountability, because it is an area in which some notable abuse has occurred. Just a few years ago, the Staff Executive of the United Way of America caused a huge scandal in this regard. In addition, I have come across some excesses – and outright dishonesty in one case – in staff expense behavior over the years through performing this review and approval function. I am pleased to report, however, that in my role of reviewing the expense accounts of Board members, who had traveled in official capacity for the organization, I never came upon any excess or dishonesty. On the contrary, they tended to be quite conservative in the expenses they submitted for reimbursement. But, regardless, some oversight is necessary relative to the expenses of Board members, too.

A final example of the carrying out of this oversight rule concerns something spoken of above under rule #1. I mentioned there that opening of donation mail everyday and making a simple record of the contents should be done in a "common area" of the office. There is no doubt that this is the most vulnerable step in the daily income process. The person assigned to this responsibility needs to know that others can see what is going on. This doesn't provide absolute security (Nothing in this whole discussion really does.), but it certainly limits the opportunity for dishonesty.

I conclude the explanation of the oversight rule with a personal observation. I always welcomed whatever oversight that members of the Board, especially its officers, wanted to offer to our organization. I certainly trusted myself. But there was comfort in knowing that others cared about the assets of the organization as much as I did.

5. Place financial assets into safekeeping as often and as quickly as possible:
The intent of this rule is clearly to protect against theft by those outside the organization. And the most obvious observance is to make bank deposits daily and as soon as they are ready. This is a responsibility that is also often ignored for reasons of convenience. But we can lessen the inconvenience by choosing a bank nearby, combining trips to the bank with other travel, or by making deposits by mail.

Other examples of appropriate safekeeping are keeping negotiable securities in safety deposit boxes, locking up supplies of blank checks and other financial instruments, and shredding discarded documents containing account numbers. There is a lot of room here for just good common sense.

6. Be aware of your most vulnerable moments and act accordingly: When thinking about this rule, the immediate circumstance from my experience that comes to mind is a fundraising special event like a run or walk at which there is a collection of cash and small checks on site. I think that this is a time when all we can do is to make the best out of a bad situation. And the "best" may be some combination of the following:

- Having at least two people at each collection station;

- Picking up proceeds from time to time and putting them in a safer location;

- Having professional security people present and visible; and

- Totaling and depositing the receipts as often and as quickly as possible.

Every organization needs to figure out for itself what its most vulnerable moments are, whether they are in being open to staff or Board dishonesty, risking theft from the outside, or just carelessness. This awareness alone is more than half of the task. Once the awareness is there, appropriate action can be taken.

7. Handle the petty cash fund properly: This seems like an obvious, perfunctory rule about a relatively small matter. But, during my career, I found that auditors usually spent some time on assessing the operation of our petty cash fund. My conclusion from this is that, in assessing how we handled relatively small financial transactions, they were able to make some judgments about how we may have handled larger transactions.

An organization's petty cash fund is structured as an impressed fund. A Board resolution authorizes it and establishes the amount of the fund, for example, in the amount of $300. Then a check is written to petty cash in that amount and given to the staff person designated as the custodian for petty cash, usually the Staff Accountant. The custodian endorses and cashes the check and puts the $300 in a safe place, usually a metal box in a locked file. Then, when another person is in need of a bit of cash, for example, to quickly purchase some supplies from a store for $20, he or she obtains the cash from the custodian and submits a bill for $20, which is then kept in the metal box. Thus, the total of the petty cash fund remains at $300, but now by $280 in cash and a paid bill for $20. And, when the actual cash in the fund gets low, for example, down to $25, a new check is issued to petty cash, but this time in the amount of $275, and this amount is expensed out into the appropriate categories. In summary, the designated custodian has the responsibility to maintain the petty cash fund at $300 at all times.

As a practical aside, in talking about a petty cash fund, I am reminded about a graduate student in one of my classes at the University of Denver's School of International Studies who commented that I needed to "get real" about these rules. He was a former Peace Corps volunteer. He stated that, while he was overseas, he and his colleagues would carry around their petty cash fund in their pockets. I was a bit flustered with his comment, but, after we all had a good laugh, we were able to conclude that he still could have followed most of these rules by considering his pocket to be a petty cash box, by keeping notes on scraps of paper about petty cash expenditures during the day, and balancing his "petty cash pocket" in the evening.

8. Purchase a fidelity bond in an appropriate amount each year: This is the last rule, and it protects the assets of the organization if all else fails. An organization purchases a fidelity bond from its property and casualty agent. Each year, when all of our insurance policies were reviewed with this agent, he or she would ask me how much exposure I felt we had to employee or volunteer theft. This is not an easy question to answer. But we would usually conclude to a round number like $50,000, and then purchase the fidelity bond in that amount for a relatively nominal fee. I am grateful that we never had to make a claim against the bond, but I always felt that this was a most worthwhile annual expenditure.

Bullet Summary

♦ The Staff Executive has the primary responsibility within a non-profit charitable organization to control financial operations and to protect its assets. He or she sets the tone for all staff and volunteers that handling financial assets properly is a very important issue in the day-to-day operation of the organization.

♦ The Board of Directors, having the ultimate fiduciary responsibility for the assets of the organization, performs a significant oversight role in financial operations. It carries out this role through its elected Treasurer, at its Board meetings, and through standing committees, such as Budget and Finance, Personnel, Audit, and Investment.

♦ There are eight recommended rules and procedures for maintaining appropriate control over financial operations and protecting the assets of the non-profit charitable organization:

1. No one person should be allowed to handle all aspects of a financial transaction.

2. All financial transactions must have adequate documentation.

3. There should be two signatures on all checks, and one of these should be of a Board member.

4. All financial operations and transactions should have regular and appropriate oversight.

5. Place financial assets into safekeeping as often and as quickly as possible.

6. Be aware of your most vulnerable moments and act accordingly.

7. Handle the petty cash fund properly.

8. Purchase a fidelity bond in an appropriate amount each year.

Conclusion

The proper control of the financial operations of a non-profit charitable organization is not accomplished without a lot of effort expended by both staff and volunteer leaders. The financial assets of the organization should be protected at all costs to provide assurance to clients and the public that the mission of the organization will be carried forward. Now we move onto the final chapter in the financial management part of this text, which addresses some important tax and some related issues faced by these non-profit organizations, even though they are tax exempt.

Suggested Readings

Konrad and Novak, op.cit., pp. 59-108.

McLaughlin, op.cit., pp. 191-207.

Chapter 6: Let's Save the Organization:

Taxes and Some Related Issues in Non-Profit Organizations

Several years ago, while driving into town on my way to the office, I heard a local morning talk show host make a plea to his listeners to make contributions to prevent a drug and youth organization from going out of business. Evidently the organization was very delinquent is depositing the Social Security and withholding taxes it had collected from and in behalf of its employees. Rather, it had been using these funds to keep its doors open. Now, as a result of all this, the organization not only lacked the funds to pay these delinquent taxes, but also was beginning to go into even more serious debt because of the penalties and interest involved. The talk show host was insisting that we needed to save this most worthwhile organization with our contributions.

Frankly, I wasn't at all moved by the host's impassioned plea. If any money is truly "not our own," then it is the money withheld from our employees' paychecks and owed in their behalf. And if a non-profit charitable organization, no matter how worthy its cause may be, cannot manage these funds properly, then I seriously doubt its ability and even integrity to manage contributed funds properly – especially mine.

This story clearly illustrates that non-profit charitable organizations, even though they are exempt from taxation in many ways, still must be concerned about taxes and tax related issues. In this chapter, I will first discuss further the withholding and transmittal responsibilities that non-profit organizations have in common with all employers. Then I will cover several related issues around the subject of tax deductibility of contributions to charitable organizations. Third, the matter of unrelated business income tax (UBIT) will be considered. Fourth, I will talk about how the Federal wage and hour laws apply to non-profit organizations. Finally, I will address the important topic of management and fundraising costs in charitable groups.

Withholding Taxes

Like all employers, non-profit charitable organizations are required by law to withhold from their employees' paychecks certain amounts for Federal and State Income Taxes and Social Security, to pay the employer's share of Social Security, and to deposit these amounts into approved accounts according to a pre-determined schedule. This all sounds simple enough. But I have seen several non-profit organizations get themselves into financial difficulty over this issue – like the one cited at the beginning to this chapter – or at least suffer the indignity of being assessed interest and penalties for being late in their required deposits. In fact, the Arthritis Foundation under my leadership was assessed in this way at least twice in my career. My only excuse was that it happened at a time when we were welcoming a new Staff Accountant to our team. (And an explanatory and repentant letter from me to the IRS resulted in a forgiveness of the penalty each time! The IRS will almost never forgive the interest.) But there really is no excuse. IRS regulations are very detailed and clear in this regard. However, these regulations change as the amount of withholding increases. So the non-profit organization needs to stay on top of the matter. It is very disheartening to have to use money, which has been donated to support the mission of a non-profit organization, to pay interest and penalties to the IRS.

Some time ago, a volunteer leader of the Arthritis Foundation at the National level offered this insight in regard to withholding taxes. He expressed the opinion that a Board member of a non-profit, who fully realizes his or her fiduciary responsibility for the financial management of the organization, can take much assurance that financial operations are being conducted properly when presented with evidence that withholding taxes are handled properly and in a timely manner. I agree with this insight.

Tax Deductibility of Contributions

In the introduction to Part A of this text, I made the point through a quote that the IRS is convinced that the Federal Treasury is being deprived of considerable income because of improper deductions taken on money given to non-profit charitable organizations. I hope that this is not true. And, above all, I hope that the organizations themselves are not misleading their contributors in this regard, either because they do not know the regulations about deductibility or because they choose not to exercise their educational responsibilities with their contributors. I believe strongly that this is an area in which non-profit charitable organizations need to be extremely conscientious. With these thoughts in mind, we will now take a look at the primary regulations about tax deductibility. Every non-profit charitable organization needs to be aware of these regulations and advise their contributors about them when it is appropriate. Unfortunately, at this point in our history, these regulations apply only to taxpayers who itemize their deductions because they exceed the standard deduction.

Total amount of deductibility: According to current tax law, donors to charitable causes can deduct from their taxable income up to 50% of their adjusted gross income in any given year. An excess of this amount can be carried over to a subsequent year. Frankly, this never became an issue for me with any donor in my career (unfortunately so!). But I can imagine that it could be a relatively common issue when dealing with exceptionally large gifts to capital campaigns and to large institutions. And perhaps this is the reason why so many of these large contributions are actually extended over a period of a few years.

Amount of deductibility for specific donations: Usually donors to charitable causes can deduct the total amount of their gifts. But, when donors receive something of value in return, the charitable organization must advise the donor that only the difference between the total amount and the value of what is received is actually deductible. The most common example of this is a fundraising special event, such as a dinner. If the charitable organization charges $100 to attend the dinner, and the dinner value is $30, then the deductible amount is $70. This would be true even if the dinner is donated by the provider or underwritten by a dinner sponsor. The regulation applies to the market value of what is being given to the donor in return, not to what the host organization actually has to pay for it. Another example would be an athletic event like a golf tournament, where the participant is charged $200 and the value of green fees, practice range, golf cart, and meals is $125. Then the donors need to be advised that the amount of charitable deduction is limited to $75.

What is the best way to advise donors about this limit on deductibility? The easiest and most effective way to do so is right on the invitation or entry form. Thus, the dinner invitation would state that, of the $100 charge to attend, $70 is tax deductible. What the donor actually does with this information is up to him or her, but we will have fulfilled our responsibility in a most effective way.

A related situation concerns donations of $250 or more. Up to a few years ago, a cancelled check issued to a charitable organization was sufficient evidence to document deductible contributions in any amount. Now this applies only to donations under $250. For donations of this amount and above, also required is a written letter or receipt issued by the charitable organization. And this letter or receipt must clearly state whether the donor received anything of value in return or not and what that value actually is in dollars. In the practical order, most direct contributions do not result in something of value being received in return. Exceptions to this would be the fundraising special events mentioned above and the fundraising campaigns, usually associated with public television and radio, which provide various premiums for different levels of giving. In any event, we fulfill our legal responsibility by including the required verbiage in our letters and receipts, and we make friends with our donors by giving them the information they need to document their tax deductions.

In-kind contributions: Donors to charitable organizations can also deduct the market value of their in-kind contributions, such as clothing, food, automobiles, art work, and the like. (Unfortunately, they cannot deduct the value of their donated time, but only their out-of-pocket costs involved with their time.) It is not our responsibility to determine this value for the donors, but we certainly can advise them to do so. In the process, we can remind them that, if their estimate of market value is $5,000 or more, the IRS requires that they document this value with an independent appraisal.

Unrelated Business Income Tax (UBIT)

It is not a true statement that non-profit charitable organizations are exempt from income taxes. On the contrary, if and when these organizations generate regular income from activities that are judged to be unrelated to their exempt purpose, then they are liable to pay taxes on their net profit. And, whenever charitable organizations carry on regular activities that generate unrelated business income, they are required to file Form 990-T along with their Form 990 annual IRS filing, regardless of whether or not they have generated a net profit from these activities.

I have observed over the last several years of my professional career that there is a growing tendency among non-profit charitable organizations to search for and actually implement unrelated, for-profit business activities. They do this to create additional income for their charitable purposes and to decrease their reliance upon contributions and other traditional sources of income. Frankly, I have never been a great fan of this trend, largely because I believe that it runs the frequent risk of causing the organization to be distracted from its central mission. Also, we risk causing resentment in the small business community, which may consider such activities on our part to be unfair competition. And, as will be pointed out in Part B of this text, I think that we can solve our income problems more effectively and efficiently by developing a strong, diversified fundraising program. But there are several leaders in the field who disagree with me in this matter, and I cannot argue the fact that the trend towards increased efforts to create unrelated business income is very real.

The best way to explain the implications of unrelated business income tax (UBIT) is to talk about a few examples. But, even with these examples, I recommend that an organization should get specific legal determination on the issue before it implements any regular activity that may result in UBIT.

A first example comes from my experience with the Arthritis Foundation. For many years we operated an Arthritis Craft Shop, in which volunteers trained people disabled with arthritis in crafts as a therapy. Their craft products were then offered for sale in the shop, and a share of the sales income was returned to the disabled worker. Because the sales proceeds were judged to be unrelated business income to the Arthritis Foundation, we always filed a Form 990-T each year. But we never paid UBIT on the revenue, because our expenses of running the shop always exceeded the income, and thus we never realized any net income on which to pay taxes. In fact, the actual net loss became so great over time that we eventually had to close the program, realizing that the expense could be spent in other ways to benefit even more people with arthritis.

Another example is a very common one. Non-profit charitable organizations often carry on occasional fundraising activities, such as garage sales or auctions. These business activities appear to be unrelated to the mission of most charitable organizations. In fact, they are. But, unless the non-profit organization operates them on a "regular" basis, the revenue from them is not considered to be subject to UBIT. Nor is the filing of a Form 990-T required.

A final example is really a classic one. As we all know, a major source of income for the Girl Scouts of America is the annual cookie sale. Selling cookies on such a regular basis and on such a grand scale – every year over a period of several weeks – would certainly appear to be a situation in which the revenue would be subject to UBIT. But, several years ago, the Girl Scout organization argued in tax court that the revenue from the annual cookie sale was actually related income. And, much to the chagrin of the IRS, the Girl Scouts won the case. The argument that swayed the court was the contention that the annual cookie sale taught girl scouts the skills of marketing and selling and, as such, fostered the mission of the Girl Scouts of America.

These examples illustrate pretty clearly when UBIT applies and when it does not. But as stated before, it is wise to secure a legal determination in the matter before engaging in business activities that may or may be subject to UBIT. And, even if a non-profit charitable organization does have considerable revenue that is subject to UBIT, it does not place its 501(c)(3) tax exempt status into jeopardy as long as it actually pays the required taxes and the revenue producing activities do not become so dominant that they change the charitable nature of the organization.

Federal Wage and Hour Laws

Federal wage and hour laws regulate two issues for every employer, both non-profit and for-profit. The first issue is the minimum wage; the second is the necessity to pay overtime wages to certain employees in certain circumstances. I have never known minimum wage laws to be troublesome to non-profit organizations. But I have often seen violations of overtime regulations in such organizations, usually resulting from a lack of understanding of the applicability of the laws. And this lack of understanding usually centers around the use of compensatory time and the legal responsibility to pay overtime wages of 1 and ½ times the hourly rate.

The current hour laws, revised in August of 2004, first require every employer to classify its employees into two categories, exempt and non-exempt. An **exempt** employee is one for whom the employer is not required to pay overtime wages or give compensatory time off, regardless of how many hours are worked. He or she can be classified as exempt provided that he or she earns a salary of at least $23,600 per year (This amount is adjusted from time to time.) and is employed in one of the following three categories: executive, supervisor (one whose primary duty is to manage at least two other people), professional, or outside sales representative. All other employees are **non-exempt** and, as such, are legally entitled to overtime pay whenever they work more than 40 hours in a given workweek. The only exception is to give the non-exempt employee compensatory time off **within the same week** in which the overtime hours were worked. For example, if a non-exempt employee is required to work two extra hours on Monday, he or she can be granted two hours off on any other day of the same week. Once the workweek has ended and compensatory time off has not been given, then the non-exempt employee must be paid the required overtime rate for the extra hours.

I have found much confusion in non-profit charitable organizations about the applicability of these laws in regard to both exempt and non-exempt employees. Because there are possible severe legal and financial consequences to the failure to observe the laws in regard to non-exempt employees, we will discuss this first. Many non-profit organizations appear to not pay overtime wages to any employees, whether they are exempt or not. Instead they may grant compensatory time to all employees, oftentimes allowing them to extend their vacations or take the time off at a later date beyond the current workweek. What adds to the confusion is that the non-exempt employees may actually enjoy this option. But there is real danger here. If, for example, the employees becomes disgruntled because they are terminated, demoted, or suffer some other disagreeable action, they may file a suit against the employer on the grounds that they did not receive overtime pay when they were eligible for it. Thus, we are left with only one viable option for non-exempt employees, and that is to follow the letter of the law in regard to overtime hours that we require of them. Of course, we can reduce the expense of following the law by limiting overtime hours as much as possible with this class of employees.

Confusion about the applicability of the hour laws to exempt employees is oftentimes found in the minds of the employees themselves. They often feel that employers are required by law to give them compensatory time off when they work more than 40 hours a week. But, as was discussed above, the law simply does not apply to them. Thus, in reality, employers do not have to pay overtime or grant compensatory time to exempt employees, no matter how many hours they may require of them. However, an enlightened employer certainly realizes that some recognition should be given to exempt employees who put in hours above and beyond the demands of a regular workweek. I recommend that non-profit charitable organizations structure some compensatory time off plan for exempt employees out of fairness and to maintain a high level of staff morale and productivity.

Management and Fundraising Costs

The final issue to be addressed in this chapter is a bit unrelated to the others, but, because of its significance, it must be discussed before I conclude this part of the text on financial management. All non-profit charitable organizations have management and fundraising costs. Otherwise they could not function. Good management and effective fundraising must be supported with money. But not many donors, whether they are individuals or granting organizations, enjoy the fact that their funds are supporting management and fundraising activities. On the contrary, they usually want to support the service programs of charitable organizations. And the charitable organizations themselves, given the fact that they are mission driven, want as much of their money as possible to be spent on their programs. For these reasons, we need to keep our management and fundraising costs at a reasonable level.

But what is a reasonable level? Over the years, it has become generally accepted that management and fundraising costs together should be kept within 25% of total organization expenses. This is true both among funding groups, such as United Ways and the Combined Federal Campaign, and among "watchdog" groups, such as the Better Business Bureau. I believe that this is a reasonable standard. It allows us to support management and fundraising functions with sufficient amounts, and yet keeps our programs in proper focus as the reason for our existence.

I have witnessed several difficulties relative to this 25% standard in my career, however. The first is that many people miss-associate all costs related to salaries with management. And then, when they see that salary costs of a particular organization are around 65% of its overall expenses – which is often the case – they immediately and erroneously conclude that the organization's management costs are exorbitantly high. They fail to understand that the vast majority of this salary expense supports staff members that are working in the programs of the organization. Therefore, the salary expense for these staff members is allocated to their respective programs and not to management. I know of no other way to correct this misunderstanding than to educate people about it whenever it surfaces.

Another difficulty concerns the appropriate estimation of fundraising costs in activities that may have multiple purposes. For example, a charitable organization may conduct a mail campaign in which the primary purpose may be fundraising, but also has many program aspects in that it is alerting the community about the services of the organization and/or about the seriousness of the problems that the organization is addressing. In this case, it is legitimate to allocate costs to both fundraising and programs. The most proper way to do this is to make an honest estimate of the percentage of verbiage in the written communication that is devoted to program versus fundraising and to make a financial allocation based upon that percentage.

Still another difficulty is about the accurate allocation of salary costs across management, fundraising, and programs. Salary costs often represent the majority of expense in many non-profit organizations, as was pointed out above. Thus, the accuracy of this allocation becomes paramount. What complicates the matter is that staff members, especially in smaller organizations, oftentimes spend significant time in more than one functional area. This was certainly true in my career. We addressed it by asking staff to do periodic time studies. During randomly selected periods of each year, usually one week of each quarter, staff members would complete a special form at the end of each day allocating their work time to the various activities of the organization. Based upon the summation of these periodic studies, we could then allocate all salary costs for the year. The only problems that surfaced in this periodic time study process involved the shortsightedness of some staff members in not seeing that their work lives may have overlapped into different areas. This was especially true with fundraisers, who tended to record all of their time as fundraising, even though a considerable amount of time of any effective fundraiser is spent in the program education of actual and potential donors. This also happened with program people, who failed to perceive when their daily work carried over into the fundraising or management areas. For this reason, I carefully reviewed the times studies of each staff person before I sent them on to the Staff Accountant to make the appropriate salary allocations. When I noticed obvious shortsightedness as described here, I would ask the staff people involved to reconsider their time allocations. I gave such careful attention to this matter, not only because it affected the allocation of the major expense of salaries, but also because it affected the allocation of many other general costs, such as those for occupancy, telephone, and office supplies.

The final difficulty with management and fundraising costs concerns the fact that frequently some non-profit organizations' expenses for these activities may justifiably exceed 25% at various times. This is especially true at the early stages in the history of organizations or when they may be expending extra efforts in fundraising. At such times, organizations must be clear to themselves and to others that the situation is a temporary one. They also need to be ready to respond to potential individual donors and funding groups, who may object to this apparent excess, with strong arguments that give reasons for the temporary situation and with their plans to rectify it in the near future. I have found that, if the explanation offered is understandable and stresses the temporary nature of the situation, most donors and funding groups will not refuse support for this reason alone.

Bullet Summary

♦ Non-profit charitable organizations, even though they are exempt from taxation on their regular income, still have responsibilities for withholding tax deposits and social security payments from their employees' paychecks, paying the employer's share of social security in behalf of their employees, and transmitting all of these funds to the IRS in a timely fashion. If they do not, they will accrue severe penalties and interest from the IRS.

♦ Non-profit organizations need to educate their donors about the specific deductibility of their contributions, both cash and in kind.

♦ Non-profit charitable organizations do have to pay income tax on any net revenue that falls into the category of unrelated business income.

♦ Non-profit organizations, just as all employers, must follow federal wage and hour laws in regard to paying the minimum wage, overtime payments for their non-exempt employees, and compensatory time off.

♦ It is a standard in the industry for non-profit charitable organizations to keep their management and fundraising costs within 25% of their total expenses.

Conclusion

Non-profit charitable organizations need to carry out their legal responsibilities in regard to taxation and federal law. This is an important aspect of their fiduciary role and accountability to the general public, their donors, their clients, and their staffs.

This completes Part A of the text. Now we will move on to the other aspect of money that is equally as important to charitable organizations, that is the implementation of an effective and diverse money raising program that is essential to the mission fulfillment of these organizations.

Suggested Reading

Konrad and Novak, op.cit., pp. 135-148.

PART B: **RAISING MONEY THAT IS NOT YOUR OWN**

It's been my frequent experience to see that Staff Executives and Board members of non-profit charitable organizations find fundraising to be an insurmountable challenge. They fully realize that they need an effective fundraising program if they are to achieve their mission, to which they are intensely dedicated. But they do not like to ask for money, and frequently they do not know how. Therefore, this part of the text will not only talk about how to raise money effectively, but also will address head on the aversion to asking for money that is present in so many leaders of charitable organizations.

The key to building an effective fundraising program is a thorough understanding of the world of philanthropy in the United States. Fortunately, there is an organization that continually keeps us up to date on this subject. It is the Giving USA Foundation. Every year it gathers data on charitable giving in our country and publishes a full report, containing information on the total amount of donations, the sources of these, the recipients, and trends over many years. For example, "Giving USA 2008" indicated that there was a total of $306.39 billion in charitable contributions in the year 2007. That is a surprisingly high figure to most people. But what is even more surprising is from where this large amount actually came. The same report for 2007 states that 74.8% of the total amount came from individuals; 7.6% came from bequests; 12.6% came from foundations; and 5.1% came from corporations. When we consider that all bequest income comes from individuals, too, we are left with the conclusion that a whopping 82.4% of all philanthropic giving in the United States came from individuals. And giving from individuals has continually been in the neighborhood of 83% of the total for at least 40 years.

This is always a surprise – even a shock – to my graduate students when I begin the course on fundraising with data like these. And, despite these clear and overwhelming data, I have found that many non-profit charitable organizations devote the majority of their fundraising efforts to foundations and other grant making organizations – which, indeed, should be a significant component of the overall fundraising program – but oftentimes devote little effort to building a development program centered on raising money from individuals. For this reason, and because of the evidence provided yearly by the Giving USA Foundation, the major portion of the fundraising part of this text will be devoted to raising money effectively from individuals.

Before concluding this introduction to Part B of the text, I want to share some additional data from the Giving USA Foundation that have real implication for the building of a successful fundraising program in non-profit charitable organizations. "Giving USA 2008" reports that religion received about 33.4% of charitable gifts in 2007. This, too, is a relatively constant percentage over the last many years. This fact should not be a surprise, given that most churches do center their fundraising efforts around individuals and effectively ask for contributions regularly, if not every week. Other significant causes that benefited in 2007 from the generosity of the American people are health (7.6%), education (14.1%), human services (9.7%), arts and culture (4.5%), the environment and animals (2.3%), and international affairs (4.3%). These percentages do change from year-to-year, but they never challenge religion for pre-eminence.

Another significant fact to be garnered from the "Giving USA 2008" report is that fundraising in the United States shows a steady increase year-after-year despite downturns in the economy. At worst, the trend line indicates a slight flattening in fundraising results during periods of economic recession. For example, the report shows only a slowing down in the growth of fundraising during the recession years in the early 70's, early 80's, and early 90's, while a real flattening only happened in the late 60's and early 2000's. Clearly, however, the U.S. economy is currently facing a greater slump than any of these, and it is too early to conclude to the overall impact of this severe predicament on our country's philanthropy. But, despite some dire predictions on the part of some, I suspect that the positive historical pattern will continue – buoyed up by the inherent generosity of the American people.

A final item of data from the Giving USA Foundation that will influence the second part of this text is that total charitable giving in the United States continually represents about 2% of the gross national product (GNP). I find this fact to be discouraging because, in effect, there seems to be no "real" growth in charitable giving, at least in a relative sense. We just seem to be "stuck" at 2% of our GNP. This certainly causes the total amount of philanthropy to grow in most years and to show a steady increase over time, but I still see a real challenge here. It seems to me that, if we can improve our fundraising methods significantly and do a much better job of appealing to the inherent generosity of the American people, we can break out of this pattern and raise substantially more money for the causes we believe in so strongly. Hopefully, the second part of this book responds to this challenge, even in a small way.

Chapter 7: I Don't Like to beg:

A Conceptual Approach to Fundraising in Non-Profit Organizations

Many years ago we hired a young, energetic, and bright Special Events Coordinator for our Chapter of the Arthritis Foundation. Let's call her Sally. She was terrific at organizing and implementing special events. Sally was very detail oriented, and she had the knack of bringing together people and arrangements to conduct a most enjoyable event. Everyone, especially volunteers, seemed to like her and to be working with her. However, over the two to three years that she worked with us, the special events she was in charge of didn't result in very much money being raised. Her supervisor pointed out this problem to her often, and encouraged her to do much better at obtaining financial sponsorships for the events long before their actual occurrence. Sally's response to this encouragement was something like this: "I'm not good at that because I don't like to beg." We worked with her for a long time, trying to help her overcome her obvious aversion to doing what was required of her, especially because she had so many other truly useful skills. But she was unable to become comfortable in actually asking for money, or even in helping volunteers in their efforts to do so. As a result, we reluctantly had to let Sally go.

This real life story illustrates clearly the necessity to have an appropriate conceptual approach to fundraising if we want to be successful at it. Sally's association of fundraising with begging created such an aversion in her that she could not do what she had to do. Many staff and volunteers in non-profit charitable organizations have similar thoughts about fundraising, and, as a result, refuse to be involved in this unpleasant task – at least in their minds – or do so only with great reluctance and slowness. That is why the primary focus of this first chapter on fundraising is on an appropriate conceptual approach. This is the necessary first step in the building of an effective fundraising program.

With these thoughts in mind, the chapter will proceed as follows. First, I will present an historical overview of philanthropy in the United States. Then, I will list some positive aspects of fundraising, to counteract its bad image in so many people's minds. Third, we will look at fundraising as a voluntary exchange among people. After that, I will explain that the most successful fundraising programs are based upon building a loyal base of contributing constituents. Fifth, we will consider the emerging profession of fundraising and its importance to non-profit organizations. Then, we will discuss the differing and complementary roles of Board Members and Staff in fundraising. And, finally, I will define a complete, diversified fundraising program and explain its importance.

An Historical Overview of Philanthropy in the United States

There are usually several graduate students from other countries in my classes in the International School at the University of Denver. These students oftentimes have had little or no experience with philanthropy in their own countries and have some difficulty in comprehending it. On the contrary, they are familiar with higher tax rates than in the United States and with governments that attempt to do more for their citizens than our government does in this country. Thus, at least in regard to the role of philanthropy in society, there is a fundamental difference between the United States and many other countries.

Philanthropy is the voluntary sharing of personal resources, financial and in kind, to promote the well being of others. For a whole complex of historical reasons, it has found a real home in the United States and continues to thrive. And it has been the driving force in the tremendous growth of non-profit organizations or the third sector in our country, which, as mentioned in the first half of this text, is perhaps our greatest gift to the world.

What are a few of these historical reasons? First and foremost is the motivation of many of the early immigrants to this country. They fled from forms of government that were judged by them to be inadequate and/or oppressive. They came with an inherent mistrust of such governments to meet their needs. As a result, they tended to pool their resources to fulfill their needs. So, when they needed health care, they raised the funds to build and operate health facilities to meet this need. When they wanted higher education, they did the same. Such motivation led to the establishment of some major hospitals, private universities, and many other charitable organizations in our country, many of which still exist to this day.

Another reason is the tax structure of this country. A dislike for taxes is deep seated in the American people. As evidence of this, we have one of the lowest tax burdens in the industrialized world. And it is the rare political candidate that can advocate increasing taxes, for whatever cause, and still be elected. In recognition of this reality, our tax laws actually encourage people to be philanthropic through a reduction in taxes for individuals and businesses that make charitable donations. Implied in this practice is a belief that charitable contributions support community activities that otherwise would have to be provided by government. One can argue, of course, that this system does not allow us to satisfy the needs of our citizens in a comprehensive, fully organized way. But conducting this argument here, as stated before, is beyond the scope of this book. I speak of our tax structure and how it affects charitable giving only as a reality with which we have to deal.

A final reason to discuss here for the high level of philanthropy in the United States probably relates to the first reason mentioned above concerning the motivation of early immigrants to this country. It is the strong and constant tendency of American people with common interests to come together and form organizations to accomplish their mutual goals in a private, voluntary way. These common interests could be human rights, gun ownership concerns, animal welfare, the environment, or neighborhood improvement. And, if the founders of these various organizations are successful in generating a broader public interest in their causes, they will conduct fundraising campaigns to support their activities. Thus, new motivations and targets for personal charitable giving are created almost every day.

The association between voluntarism and charitable giving has always been of great interest to me. According to studies conducted frequently by the Independent Sector and entitled "Giving and Volunteering in America," it has been verified over and over again that over half of the households in America have people in them who volunteer for something. (This, too, is a cause for amazement among many of my graduate students from other countries.) The other related and consistent finding of these studies is that over 80% of charitable giving comes from households in which there are volunteers. This clearly says something meaningful about the American people. A substantial number of our people not only financially contribute to the causes they judge to be important, but also give of themselves and their time to further these causes.

I believe that we can conclude from all of this that charitable giving is a major force in the United States. It has been with us for a very long time, is supported by historical circumstances and our laws, distinguishes us from many other countries, is associated with our voluntary spirit, and is so deeply rooted that it will continue to thrive. Given this reality, it's time for the volunteer and staff leaders of non-profit charitable organizations to overcome the aversion to fundraising that they may have, to quit delegating this major responsibility to only a few, and to truly get involved in an activity that flows from something inherent and even beautiful in the American people.

Positive Aspects of Fundraising

Early in my professional career, I had many negative views about fundraising. For whatever reason and wrongly so, I had little respect for the few professional fund-raisers that I knew. And even when I applied and was hired to be the Staff Executive of the Arthritis Foundation, I didn't realize that it was primarily a fundraising job. In fact, this was hardly discussed in the interview process. But, once on the job, it didn't take me long to figure out that my bottom line responsibility was fundraising. Given the ultimate goal of the organization – to rid the world of the devastation of arthritis – and realizing that this would happen only by medical research promoted and supported by contributed dollars, I then knew that I was to lead an effort for which I was not previously trained. So, through attendance at national meetings of the Foundation, personal reading, talking with others involved in fundraising, and lots of trial and error, I gradually learned what fundraising was all about. Moreover and much to my surprise, I learned to actually like and enjoy it. But why?

First of all, up to then in my career I was never really certain that my hard work in previous positions had ever really made a difference to anyone. I really didn't know whether I was successful or not. But I soon found out that fundraising is very differ-ent in this regard. In a fundraising program, the people involved establish a specific financial goal for themselves, work hard to reach that goal, and then definitely know whether they reach that goal or not. And, when they do reach the goal – or come reasonably close – there is a tremendous feeling of accomplishment. I enjoyed this sense of accomplishment. I also enjoyed knowing when we were not successful; at least the outcome was definite, and we could make immediate plans to do much better the next time.

But that was not all. I could then see clearly the difference the funds raised made in the lives of people we served. Those funds made it possible for us to establish and maintain valuable services for people with arthritis and to support medical research that was producing results almost every day in medical centers around the country. What really sold me on the value of fundraising, however, was the difference it made in the lives of the donors themselves. Seeing their joy and sense of accomplishment in giving was a surprising revelation to me. Then I knew that I was engaged in something truly worthwhile. For the rest of my career, I found much satisfaction in providing the leadership for our fundraising program and in being personally involved in it. I was proud to say that I was a professional fundraiser. Fundraising no longer presented a negative image to my mind.

A Voluntary Exchange among People

The first step in the development of an appropriate appreciation for fundraising is realizing what it is – and what it is not. The writing of the late Henry A. Rosso helped me to gain this realization more than anything else. Rosso, besides being a professional fundraiser throughout his long career, was the founding director of The Fund Raising School at Indiana University in 1974. (Up until just a few years ago, this was the only educational institution in the country from which one could obtain an academic degree in fundraising.) In his writing, Rosso stresses the following points: Fundraising is not an end to itself; it is an exchange transaction and not begging; it is voluntary and, therefore, can be destroyed by coercion; and it functions best when the needs of the charitable organization are matched perfectly by the donor's need to give. (1) Let's look closely at each of these points.

Fundraising is not an end in itself: What this means is that the justification for raising money is never found in the dollars themselves, but in the goal or mission for which the dollars are raised. This clearly differentiates fundraising from sales, where the ultimate objective for both the company and the salesperson is the resulting profit. Thus, fundraising is in a subsidiary position to its purpose. And, if its purpose is not truly worthwhile, then it is meaningless, no matter how successful it may be. That is why a clear, compelling statement of the purpose of a fundraising program is the required first step in the process. If this is not done, not only will the chance of fundraising success be severely limited because of insufficient motivation for donors, but also the volunteers and staff involved in the process will find little satisfaction in their efforts.

Fundraising is an exchange transaction and not begging: To say the same thing in different words, in fundraising **both** the charitable organization and the donor receive something meaningful. That is why the organization and especially the people involved in the asking are not beggars. They have as much to offer the prospective donor as the donor has to offer the organization. What the organization receives is clear; it is the financial support for its mission. But what the donor receives is not so clear; it might be as simple as some personal satisfaction. However, almost always it is more complex than that. For this reason, it is critical for the recipient organization to find out the real motivation for the donor's generosity.

In this context, I am reminded of a clever article written several years ago by Robert Hartsook, entitled "77 Reasons Why People Give" and published in the professional journal, Fund Raising Management. (2) Dr. Hartsook lists 77 reasons why people respond positively to fundraising appeals. Examples are:

2. They know their gifts will make a difference.

8. They feel it's their duty.

9. You allow them to relieve guilt…..

15. They believe it is a blessing to do so.

18. You give them the opportunity to "belong" to something as a member, friend or supporter.

29. You aid them in doing something for a family member, a friend, a child or grandchild.

37. They respect the leaders of the organization.

Of course, there are many more than 77 reasons why people make charitable contributions. These 77 are all generic in nature. Many more reasons flow from the specific nature of the mission involved and the particular needs of the donors.

The point here is that, if fundraising is an exchange transaction, it is incumbent upon the charitable organization to try to find out the particular motivations of each donor as it builds a relationship with him or her. Then the organization can make reference to these motivations in future communications and appeals and, thus, do its part in the exchange.

Fundraising is voluntary and, therefore, can be destroyed by coercion: The voluntary nature of the charitable contribution distinguishes it from taxation and gives it nobility. We are appealing to the very best in people when we ask for a contribution. That is why coercion is so out of place in a fundraising program. When we use coercion in any of its forms, we rob people of their opportunity to be truly noble and generous. And their response will be limited in nature, and our chances of obtaining repeat gifts are certainly diminished.

What are some examples of coercion? I often ask my graduate students this question. These are a few of their responses:

> 1. When an employer, especially the boss, exerts so much pressure to give to a charitable campaign (for example, the annual United Way drive) that the employee is made to feel that his or her job may be at stake.

> 2. When a young student in the neighborhood appears on a doorstep selling candy or other items to support school activities.

> 3. When a religious leader attempts to create a high sense of obligation or duty in an institutional fundraising appeal.

Clearly, these are all worthwhile causes. In most cases, too, the charity itself does not wish to use coercion. Rather the coercion flows from the over-zealousness of the ones making the appeal. Nonetheless, it is coercion. And, even though the immediate result may be an actual contribution, it is usually minimal and, most importantly, gives no real satisfaction to the donor.

Most successful fundraisers and fundraising organizations understand the voluntary nature of the charitable contribution. They avoid using coercion in any form. Rather, they give people an opportunity to make a difference, to be generous and caring, or to be part of something much bigger than themselves. As a result, when people do respond, as they often do if these opportunities are presented to them effectively, they do so with a generous spirit and receive a great deal of satisfaction in return.

Fundraising functions best when the needs of the charitable organization are matched perfectly by the donor's need to give: This is a real mouthful. And it says a lot. The best way I know to explain it is to give two examples drawn from my fundraising career. The first is about a middle aged professional woman who gave regular gifts of $500 or so to the Arthritis Foundation. When I asked her why she gave such generous annual gifts, she responded that she did so out of gratitude for the fact that an arthritis specialist she went to see had explained to her, after a thorough examination, that she actually did not have arthritis, but another illness that was more readily treated. She was actually thanking that doctor when she made her thoughtful contributions to the Arthritis Foundation. And one year she made a donation of several thousand dollars without us ever having asked her to do so!

The second example is of an elderly widow who was confined to her home because of serious arthritis, under constant nursing care. She made regular annual gifts of several thousand dollars to the Arthritis Foundation. Despite her physical disability, her mind was exceedingly sharp, and I truly enjoyed my regular visits to her home, primarily done to express gratitude for her generosity. She often expressed her wish that others would not have to suffer with arthritis as she did. But one day she went even further than this. As I left that day, she said emphatically: "Ted, when I'm down to my last nickel, I'll share it with you!" (Of course, she was referring to the Arthritis Foundation, not to me personally.)

In both of these examples, the donors had a specific need to make a charitable contribution, and the Arthritis Foundation represented a perfect match for that need. The more that non-profit charitable organizations can identify donors who have needs to give that match perfectly with their respective missions, the more successful they will be in their fundraising programs to advance those missions.

There is no doubt that it takes time to identify these matches between donors and charitable organizations. And most likely it is easier to do so in an organization like the Arthritis Foundation with a very focused and non-controversial cause. However, the "time" issue can only be resolved by commitment of existing staff and volunteers, or by the allocation of new resources to hire and/or recruit new staff or volunteers, to spend the time to learn about the specific motivations of donors. But how does an organization, which has difficulty in making such identification – like a grass roots and controversial advocacy organization, for example – go about doing this? I know of no other way than dogged determination to begin talking with a few donors, who appear to be more generous and/or regular in their contributions, to learn about their specific motivations for engaging in these controversial activities. What is gained from such efforts will be truly invaluable. First, the current generous donors will feel more personal satisfaction and will very probably increase their support. Second, the charitable organization will learn a great deal about how to reach out more effectively to others to either begin new relationships and receive new contributions or to intensify and increase contributions from existing donors that they do not know very well.

__Fundraising is a voluntary exchange among people:__ I wish to add one final point to those made by Rosso. It flows from his points mentioned and explained above, and is actually a summary of all of his points. We've talked about fundraising being "voluntary" and an "exchange." Now I want to stress that it happens "among people." By this I mean that the fundraising transaction usually and most effectively happens on a deeply personal level, or person-to-person. A person who represents a non-profit charitable organization asks another person, who most often represents only himself or herself but sometimes a funding entity, to support the charitable organization, and this other person responds favorably largely because of the personal relationship that exists between the two of them. That is why I believe – and my experience has confirmed this over and over again – that the level of personalism involved in a fundraising program is a powerful determinant of the success of that program. It is a more powerful determinant than the number of the fundraising requests per year or the quality of the media used in the requests. The full implications of this statement will be seen more clearly in later chapters when we discuss the actual methods of fundraising.

Constituent-Based Fundraising

The most successful fundraising organizations focus their efforts on the identification of a natural group of constituents, building an on-going relationship with this group, reaching out beyond the members of this group to others related to the members, and, all the while, effectively asking the members of the group as it expands to give their support on an on-going basis. That is why the most significant recipient of charitable dollars in this country by far, as pointed out in the introduction to this part of the text, is religion. Religious groups – at least the most thriving ones from a monetary point of view – have become very skilled in building a loyal group of constituents, in continually expanding the numbers of this group, and in regularly asking this group for its support. All non-profit charitable organizations can improve on their fundraising capacities by imitating religious groups in this regard.

I try to illustrate this concept in the classroom by drawing a series of concentric circles on the blackboard. In the center are the individuals who are naturally very close to the mission of the charitable organization and to its day-to-day operation. These are the members of the Board, the staff, principal donors, and regular clients of the organization. All of these people can reach out to others in their acquaintance to bring them into the wider circles of the organization, and then these others can be asked to use their influence to bring even others into the constituency of the organization. In this way, a non-profit charitable organization can create and maintain an ever-expanding group of constituents who are in the circle of the organization, who identify with its mission, and who support it financially on a regular basis. In a word, it is now "their" organization.

What helps in this process is the identification of potential supporters who have a natural affinity for the organization. For example, people with heart disease and their families have a natural affinity for the Heart Association; college alumni have a natural affinity for their college; and neighborhood residents have a natural affinity for the community center in their neighborhood. It is much easier to reach out to and effectively invite people with affinity to become part of a constituent group than to reach out to the general public. So the first challenge is to identify those people with affinity. I agree that this is more difficult for some organizations than others. But I submit that almost every charitable organization has a significant number of potential constituents because otherwise it simply would not exist – or perhaps should no longer exist!

Another important factor about constituent-based fundraising is that normal attrition through death, moving, decrease in income, and loss of interest causes a 20% to 30% loss of constituents on an annual basis. For this reason, the charitable organization can never rest in its efforts to bring more and more people into its constituent group. In addition, the organization needs to communicate regularly with the members of its constituent group **without** always asking for contributions. We don't want our constituents to remark: "I only hear from that organization when it wants my money!" This is the role that a regular newsletter can perform. And in these days a newsletter can be produced and sent out over the Internet very inexpensively. Such regular communications not only bring constituents closer and closer to the center of charitable organizations, they also serve to increase the response rates and amounts of donations when the requests for financial support are actually made.

The Fundraising Profession

There have been people skilled at asking for money from others for charitable purposes for a very long time in this country. But the existence of a recognized fundraising profession is a relatively recent phenomenon in our history. As evidence of this, to my knowledge, there are only two universities in the United States from which one can receive an actual degree in fundraising. These are the University of Indiana, previously mentioned, and New York University. Most people who call themselves fundraising professionals have been educated in many other disciplines, such as public relations, marketing, education, social work, and business. They have come to their current work through any number of indirect routes and have had to learn their profession on their own through reading, seminars, and mentoring. Bringing some order to this situation is the Association of Fundraising Professionals (AFP), which has a published Code of Ethics and a professional certification program (CFRE or Certified Fund Raising Executive). So we are dealing with an emerging profession, which is growing in stature and stability. It still has a long way to go, however.

Large institutions, like hospitals and universities, have employed professional fundraisers for a very long time. They are becoming more and more common in larger charitable organizations like voluntary health organizations, family service agencies, and youth-serving groups. But many small community and grass roots organizations attempt to support their operations without professional fundraisers on staff. In general, there is much room in the non-profit world for qualified fundraisers. There is even room for professional people from other disciplines to venture into this particular work if they are willing to overcome their natural aversion to it and seek out some training. And it is not at all unusual for those engaged in fundraising to be paid significantly more for their labors than other professionals in the same organizations because of these market considerations.

This leads me to point out a severe current problem that the fundraising profession needs to solve for itself. The problem results from the high demand for qualified fundraising professionals joined with the qualities of an effective fundraising program described earlier in this chapter. As stated before, fundraising is a "voluntary exchange among people." It isn't accomplished without real and sustained efforts at relationship building between the charitable organizations and their donors. And this takes time! The role of the professional fundraiser is to be the coordinator of this relationship building. But how can he or she accomplish this while moving from one organization to another every few years or so? This appears to be the case in far too many instances, at least in my observation over the last several years. And there are severe negative consequences from this instability as pointed out by a recent article in the "Chronicle of Philanthropy:"

> The cost of turnover can be measured in lost gifts. A 2007 study of
> more than 1,000 fundraisers who seek big donations for colleges
> and universities, conducted by Eduventures, a Boston consulting
> company, found that fundraisers who had been in their positions

for less than five years obtained about half of the contributions
they sought. Those with more then five years on the job obtained
closer to two-thirds of the gifts they pursued. (3)

Who is to blame for this obvious problem? It's hard to blame the individual professionals involved, especially when they are offered better opportunities, even when they are not actively seeking them. It's also hard to blame the hiring organizations, which are simply trying to fill important positions. I simply point out the problem in the hope that its revelation may lead to some resolution, which can only be found in fundraising professionals being willing to make prolonged commitments to one cause and their employers being willing to support that commitment with corresponding salary increases.

To conclude this discussion about the emerging profession of fundraising, there are several positive points to make. A qualified fundraising professional can be a valuable asset – if not an essential one – to most non-profit charitable organizations. The value and success of a particular fundraising professional can be measured easily over time. The fundraising profession itself is a rewarding, satisfying one. It is in high demand and pays relatively well. The technical skills required can be learned. The qualities necessary come naturally for some, but perhaps harder for others. They are abilities to listen, to be organized, to relate well with people of all kinds, to remember important details, to be personally committed to a particular mission, to be able to encourage and help others to ask, and to not be afraid to be the one doing the asking when needed.

Complementary Roles of Board and Staff

The implementation of an effective fundraising program can only be accomplished if the members of the Board of Directors and Staff of the non-profit charitable organization work in partnership. They have distinct roles to play, and these oftentimes overlap. Let's talk first about the roles of the Board of Directors.

Roles of the Board of Directors in Fundraising: The on-going financial support for the programs of the organization is a responsibility that rests ultimately with the members of the Board of Directors, just like all other important aspects of the organization's life. As a result, their first role to be fulfilled – and perhaps their most important one – is to be financial contributors themselves. I have noticed that this primary responsibility of the Board has become more and more clarified during the many years of my career. In fact, it has become very explicit in many charitable organizations that have "give or get" policies. In other words, Board members are told that, in order to remain on the Board, they must "give" a certain amount of money each year, "get" it from someone else, or produce it through some combination of the two. Frankly, I object to such explicit policies, simply because they seem crass to me and possibly qualify as coercion. In addition, I have seen otherwise excellent Board members leave organizations when such policies are adopted. The same goal can be achieved, in a much more professional way, with an adoption of a policy that states simply and clearly something like this: "Board members are expected to financially support the organization with an annual gift that is as generous as they are able to make it." Such a policy makes it clear that a more than perfunctory gift is required, but the actual amount is left up to the individual member of the Board.

Board members have financial support responsibilities that go far beyond their own personal gifts. These responsibilities can be categorized as either leadership or direct involvement. Leadership is fulfilled through service on the Development Committee, which has the overall responsibility for planning the total fundraising program of the organization, or on other fundraising committees, such as Annual Campaign, Major Gifts, Corporate Giving, Planned Giving, or one implementing a specific special event. Direct involvement in fundraising is fulfilled when Board members actually ask individuals or other funding sources for contributions when they are judged to be the most appropriate ones to ask because of business relationships, friendships, or knowledge. Such direct involvement is the most difficult of all for most Board members that I have known. But they need to realize that they are in a strong position to be the asking person – usually in a much stronger position than staff – because they are volunteers and, as such, have nothing personal to gain in the transaction. Prospective donors know and respect this fact. And nothing overcomes a reluctance to be the asking person more than some real success, which is bound to come with sincere and intelligent effort.

Roles of staff in fundraising: All of this about the Board's primary responsibility in fundraising does not diminish the roles of staff in any way. Staff members at all levels of the charitable organization actually have indispensable roles to carry out. This is especially true for the Staff Executive, Director of Development, and other professional fundraisers, if the organization is fortunate to have them. But, to a lesser degree, it is also true for staff involved in the service and administrative functions of the organization.

First of all, just as I stated about the Board, the roles of staff members in fundraising begin with their own personal financial support – at least in my opinion. This is quite controversial and not at all accepted among many graduate students in my courses and among many professional staff people of charitable organizations with whom I have talked about the issue. (They tend to feel that their low salaries, compared to the for-profit business world, are already a contribution to the organization.) Moreover, I know of no charitable organization that requires this as a condition of employment, and rightly so. At a minimum, such a policy would be unethical, if not illegal. Nonetheless, I believe that the responsibility to give should flow logically and voluntarily from the staff members themselves. In this way, they demonstrate their personal commitment to the mission of the organization like nothing else can. And I have seen, especially in myself, the added meaning and satisfaction in charitable, professional work that flows from making a generous gift – however this may be defined by the individual staff person – to support the cause for which one is working. But, again, such staff financial contributions cannot be required in any way. All that can be done are examples set by the Staff Executive and other management staff, a bit of encouragement, and perhaps the creation of some opportunities to give.

Just as with the Board of Directors, responsibilities of staff members in fundraising go far beyond their own personal contributions. Generally speaking, their roles tend to be supportive to those of the Board and/or technical in nature. On the supportive side, they may encourage and facilitate Board members in carrying out their fundraising efforts. For example, oftentimes the most effective fundraising ask is done by a twosome of the Board member and a staff person. In this case, the Board member uses his or her influence in the situation and the staff member provides the necessary program information. On the technical side, the staff members may actually draft fundraising letters for Board member signature, produce large mailings, and handle the many details involved in a special event.

I want to give special consideration to the roles of the Staff Executive, the Director of Development, and other professional fundraisers in the money-raising program of the charitable organizations. All have leadership roles to play. And the roles of the Staff Executive are uniquely important. In my opinion, his or her involvement in fundraising is a responsibility that cannot be totally delegated. People can argue that the Staff Executive's responsibilities for strategic planning, budgeting, and mission achievement are equally as important, and they may very well be correct. But, given the significance of sufficient income for the on-going existence of the organization and the particular need for executive leadership in the attainment of fundraising success, I believe that the Staff Executive cannot afford to be very far away from the fundraising program at any time. His or her constant interest and support are essential to success in this challenging area of the organization's life. In addition, there are some fundraising objectives that only the Executive can accomplish. Sometimes prospective major donors, for example, just want to talk with the "boss" before they make any commitment. It is also becoming increasingly common for the Staff Executive to actually assume full responsibility for the cultivation of certain key contributors in the organization's major gift program. During the last several years of my executive career, I tried to devote about 25% of my time to the major gift program in this way and not only significantly increased our major gift income, but also found much personal satisfaction and enjoyment in the process.

The Director of Development and other professional fundraisers on staff definitely are the operational leaders of the fundraising program for the non-profit charitable organization. In this capacity, they must devote considerable time to the money-raising effort and be held accountable for the success or failure of this activity. But it is also important for them to demonstrate interest and on occasion to actually be involved in the other activities of the organization that are related to service and mission achievement. I suggest this for two reasons. First, they will gain a deeper understanding of the mission of the organization and, thus, become more effective fundraisers. Second, once they have shown interest in these other programs, it will be easier for them to ask for and receive the active assistance of other staff members in the fundraising effort when their assistance is needed, for example, in special events and other intensive fundraising activities at critical times.

A Comprehensive, Diversified Fundraising Program

This is the final topic to address in the chapter, and it's a very important one. Far too many non-profit charitable organizations that I have known place themselves in continual jeopardy because they do not have a comprehensive, diversified fundraising program. In other words, they are too dependent on one or two sources of funds. And, when one of these significantly diminishes or even discontinues its funding, the very existence of the organizations is at risk. Let's look at a few examples to illustrate this point.

I have seen many organizations try to maintain a certain level of financial support almost solely through foundation and government grants. What a precarious situation this is! Most foundations will not give grants to the same organization year after year, and oftentimes they change their funding priorities. And, as we have experienced over the last 30 years in particular, State and Federal funding can not only drastically decrease, it can also terminate in some areas. Such uncertainty creates a lack of confidence about the future in such dependent organizations and severely inhibits their ability to plan and to grow. I am not trying to say that foundation and government grants cannot and should not be a meaningful part of the on going funding of non-profit charitable organizations. But I do say that such grants should not dominate the financial structure of these organizations, especially considering that there is a more secure and effective way to go.

Another example is even more specific. Several years ago, I learned about a children's advocacy organization that was growing and thriving. This was largely due to the personal philanthropic interest of a notable, wealthy public figure in the area. The person's contributions and influence produced about 70% of the organization's financial support. But, in a particular year, the organization lost most of the individual's support because he had transferred his personal interest to another cause. As a result, the organization almost went out of business and struggled for many years to regain its financial footing.

A final example comes from my professional experience. When I was hired to be the Staff Executive of our Chapter of the Arthritis Foundation in 1976, the annual budget was about $200,000. Of this amount, approximately 65% came from the local United Way. I concluded that this was a dangerous situation, not only because of the over dependence on one source of funding, but also because I knew that the funding priorities of the United Way could change at any time. In addition, the organization had not been growing at all for several years. I am proud to write that, when I retired in 2001, due to the concerted planning and work of many volunteer leaders and staff, the total budget of the organization had grown to $2,500,000. United Way annual support stayed about the same, but it now represented just 4% of the total. The real growth came from the development of a comprehensive, diversified fundraising program.

But what is a comprehensive diversified fundraising program? It definitely begins with a real effort directed at building a constituent-based fundraising program as described earlier in this chapter. Another name for this is an annual giving program, which will be the subject of the next chapter. Through this program, the non-profit charitable organization identifies, reaches out to, and effectively solicits an ever-expanding group of individual donors who support the organization with their contributions year after year. Methodologies employed in the annual giving program range from direct mail, telemarketing, individual and group solicitations, and the

Internet to membership and donor club initiatives and even special events. (I mention special events in this context because of their potential to identify new annual donors from among their participants.) But the major point to be made here is that a strong annual giving program is the bedrock for all else in a comprehensive, diversified fundraising program. In other words, if this doesn't exist in an organization, there is little chance that the organization will ever be comfortable in its ability to maintain itself and to grow.

Once an effective annual giving program is in place, the non-profit charitable organization can move on to major gifts, capital campaigns, and endowments. The vast majority of donors to these higher dollar fundraising initiatives will come from the individuals already supporting the organization in the annual giving program or at least will be identified through this group. The organization can also more effectively enter into raising funds from corporations and foundations once it has the annual giving program in place. Such funders very frequently insist that the organization be able to demonstrate a broad base of community support before it will consider responding positively to contribution requests or grant applications.

The final initiative to be added to the fundraising program is one devoted to procuring bequests and other planned gifts from among its regular individual supporters. Clearly this effort is contingent upon a successful annual giving program, as was evidenced over and over again in my career. Over time, bequests and planned giving represented about 30% of our income in our Chapter of the Arthritis Foundation. And the majority of these individual donors came from among our regular supporters.

So, to sum up the definition of a comprehensive, diversified fundraising program, it is a total fundraising effort that includes annual giving, memberships, direct mail, Internet and telephone solicitation, special events, major gifts, capital, endowment, and other special campaigns, foundation grants, government grants (if appropriate), corporate giving, and bequests and planned giving. But again, if it is to be a truly successful fundraising program, it must start with the annual giving of an ever-expanding group of individual donors and always be based upon that initiative.

I believe that J. M. Greenfield developed an excellent graphic illustration of a comprehensive, diversified fundraising program, which was called a "Pyramid of Giving." I re-draft it here to conclude this chapter:

PYRAMID OF GIVING

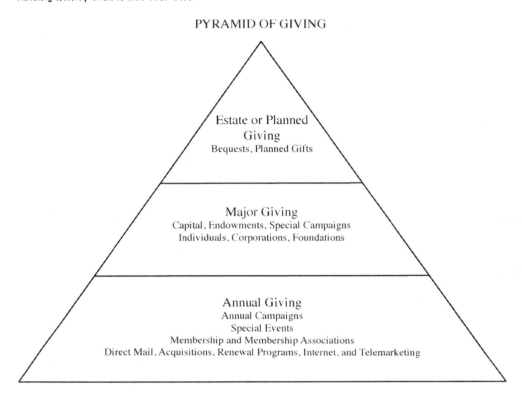

Estate or Planned
Giving
Bequests, Planned Gifts

Major Giving
Capital, Endowments, Special Campaigns
Individuals, Corporations, Foundations

Annual Giving
Annual Campaigns
Special Events
Membership and Membership Associations
Direct Mail, Acquisitions, Renewal Programs, Internet, and Telemarketing

Source: "Fund-Raising: Evaluating and Managing the Fund Development Process," J.M. Greenfield, Copyright © 1991 John Wiley & Sons, Inc.

The structure of the pyramid itself helps to drive home the points I have been making. The "Annual Giving" Program is at the base or foundation of the pyramid, with more donors giving small amounts, but being the foundation for all the rest. Then, as we move up the pyramid to "Major Giving," we have fewer donors with larger gifts. Finally, we reach the top of the pyramid to "Estate or Planned Giving," where we have even fewer donors with the largest contributions. All of us in the non-profit charitable world should strive to reach and maintain this fully developed fundraising program. If we do, we will have the required financial resources to not only survive, but, more importantly, to attain the goals and objectives implied in our missions.

Bullet Summary

◆ Charitable giving is a consistent and dominant force in the history of the United

States and is a major way for non-profit charitable organizations to support their important missions.

♦ Despite a negative view of fundraising that is shared by many leaders of non-profit organizations, there are many positive and even noble aspects of this essential activity.

♦ As a voluntary exchange among people, fundraising is a servant of charitable causes and not an end in itself; it is an exchange transaction and not begging; it is voluntary and can be destroyed by coercion; it works best when the needs of the charitable cause match perfectly with the donor's need to give; and it increases in effectiveness as the level of personalism in the transaction is increased.

♦ The most successful fundraising organizations have an ever-expanding, identifiable group of people who consider themselves to be constituents of the organizations and give their support regularly to these organizations.

♦ Fundraising is emerging as a highly skilled and recognized profession, which can be of great value to non-profit charitable organizations.

♦ Boards members and staff of charitable organizations have different and complementary roles in fundraising and need to work in partnership to build and maintain successful fundraising programs.

♦ Non-profit charitable organizations should strive to develop a comprehensive, diversified fundraising program to insure their existence over time, to carry out their missions, and to continually grow in their ability to serve their clients' needs.

Conclusion

Chapter 7 has talked at length about an appropriate conceptual approach to fundraising not only to enable non-profit charitable organizations to establish effective fundraising programs, but also to overcome the aversion to fundraising that exists in the minds of far too many volunteer and staff leaders of these organizations. Subsequent chapters in the text will define and discuss the various initiatives that are employed in effective fundraising programs. Chapter 8 covers the bedrock of a comprehensive fundraising program – the annual giving initiative.

Raising Money That is Not Your Own

(1) Henry A. Rosso, <u>Achieving Excellence in Fundraising</u>, Jossey-Bass Publishers, San Francisco, 1991, pp. 3-7.

(2) Robert F. Harstook, "77 Reasons Why People Give," <u>Fund Raising Management</u>, December 1998, pp. 18-19.

(3) Holly Hall, "Longevity's New Appeal," <u>Chronicle of Philanthropy</u>, Internet Report, March, 2009.

Suggested Reading

Burk, <u>Donor Centered Fundraising: How to Hold On to your Donors and Raise Much More Money</u>, Cygnus Applied Research, Inc., Chicago, 2003, pp. 3-11.

Ciconte and Jacob, <u>Fundraising Basics: a Complete Guide</u>, Aspen Publishers, Gaithersburg, MD, 2001, pp. 1-85.

Werther and Berman, op.cit., 185-202.

Chapter 8: **But It's Just Junk Mail:**

Annual Giving, Direct Mail, Internet, and Other Basic Fundraising Methods in Non-Profit Organizations

Oftentimes, when I begin discussing direct mail fundraising methods in my graduate school classes, students remark: "But it's just junk mail!" When they make this disparaging comment, they are reflecting a common feeling among many people that direct mail simply adds to the advertising waste that gathers in mail boxes and that is discarded in large part by the recipients. What they fail to realize is that high volume mailing is still the most economical and effective method to identify and solicit new charitable donors for non-profit charitable organizations. It may be replaced soon by the Internet for the same economical and effective reasons. But, until that day comes, operating a productive direct mail program is an important, if not essential, activity in any successful fundraising program.

This chapter is devoted to a full explanation of annual giving, which, as mentioned in the previous chapter, is the foundation of the comprehensive fundraising program that is needed by all non-profit charitable organizations if they are to maintain themselves and continually grow in their ability to carry out their important missions. Through the implementation of an annual giving initiative, the organization reaches out to identify and solicit an ever-growing number of interested people who provide support for the day-to-day operation of the organization on an on-going basis. The goal is to bind these people to the organization through a sense of loyalty. The implementation of this initiative requires a clear and compelling case for support of the organization, and I will discuss this first. Secondly, I will talk about the yearly analysis that needs to be done to evaluate the success of the annual giving program. Then I will explain the various fundraising methods employed in annual giving, namely, direct mail, telemarketing, the Internet, and person-to-person and, in the process, show how these methods relate to each other. Finally, I will add some thoughts on personalization and promptness, two characteristics of an annual giving program that will enhance its effectiveness more than any others in my opinion.

Case for Support

A case for support is a clear and compelling statement intended to motivate people to provide financial contributions to a non-profit charitable organization. It emphatically states why donations are needed, what difference they will make in people's lives, and precisely what the organization will do with the donations when they are given. It is not an actual request for donations in itself. Rather, it is primarily an internal document that clarifies for the Board of Directors, staff, and volunteers the specific reasons why contributions from the public and other sources are required and even essential and what they will do with the funds received. Once it has been developed and agreed upon by the organization's leaders, it becomes a source document upon which marketing materials and actual fundraising appeals are based. Thus, it enables the organization to give a unified message to its current and potential donors – a message that is based upon its mission and that gives the most compelling reasons why their support is needed and appreciated.

Before talking about what should be stated in a case for support, let's discuss first what should **not** be stated. It is not at all motivating for people to contribute to a charitable organization because funds are needed to reach its budget, to pay for its expenses, to eliminate its deficits, or to enable it to get out of debt. Such reasons might be very important to the organization's Board and staff. But most others need more exciting reasons than these. People want to make a difference, to do something important, to be involved in something big. Nor are most people motivated to lower their standard of living to support a charitable cause. So we need to be realistic and ask for a share of their discretionary funds rather than asking for sacrifice. (When making this point with my students, I usually mention that only saints – who are few and far between – are willing to respond to appeals for sacrifice!) So an effective case for support should avoid these relatively common mistakes.

Here is a suggested outline for a case for support:

> 1. Start with a clear and concise statement about the organization's vision (why it exists) and mission (what it does to fulfill its vision).

> 2. Explain who and how many are affected by the problem(s) addressed by your charitable organization. State how negatively these people and society are affected because of this problem or these problems.

3. Substantiate the need for your services, as described in #2, with data provided by some outside sources. For example, during my career with the Arthritis Foundation, we would often say that many millions of Americans of all ages are seriously affected by over 100 kinds of arthritis. But supporting data collected and published by the national Center for Disease Control (CDC) in Atlanta made this statement much stronger.

4. Give compelling reasons why people or funding organizations should make contributions. Explain the difference the contributions will make and how the donors themselves will receive benefit. Remember that effective fundraising is an "exchange."

5. State clearly how the organization will use the contributions. If you are seeking general operating support, say so. If the gifts will be used for specific purposes, state what these are. If you wish to encourage donors to designate their gifts for program areas that particularly interest them, say this, too. However, an annual giving program is usually intended to provide the general operating support on an on-going basis that is a critical need for most non-profit charitable organizations.

Before ending this discussion about a case for support, I wish to repeat the point I made in the beginning. The case for support is an internal document intended to get and keep the Board, staff, and volunteers on the same page before and during their efforts to seek significant funds from the donor public. Ideas expressed in the case can and should be used in fundraising letters and other appeals for funds. But the case is not all that is needed to conduct a successful annual giving program. The organization still needs to effectively ask potential donors to give their contributions.

Yearly Analysis of the Annual Giving Program

A successful annual giving program can never remain static. One reason for this is the inevitable attrition in annual donors that always occurs, usually about 25%, caused by death, moving, loss of interest, and change of circumstances. Another reason is the constant need to actually increase the number of annual donors and amounts of their contributions each year. So a plan needs to be in place to continually grow the annual giving program, not only to keep up with the normal costs of doing business, but also to actually increase the services and the reach of the non-profit charitable organization.

The first step in the development of such a plan is an annual analysis of the operation of the annual giving program that addresses the following questions:

1. How many annual donors did we have this year, and what was the total amount of their contributions?

2. How do these numbers compare with last year, and did we meet our goals for this year?

3. How many former donors did we lose, and how many new donors did we acquire?

4. How many donors did we have at various gift levels, for example, $10, $25, $50, $100, $250, $500? How do these numbers compare to last year?

5. The last set of questions is probably the most important of all. Who among our current donors are capable of increasing their support? Are there some that should be considered for "graduation" into our major giving program?

Armed with the information gathered through this analysis, an organization can now make specific plans to conduct the annual giving program for the following year, set new goals, and make program modifications to achieve the new goals.

Methods Used in the Annual Giving Program

With these introductory thoughts in mind, we can now move to the specific methods that are utilized in a successful annual giving program. These are direct mail, telemarketing, the Internet, and person-to-person. An organization should actually use all of these methods and relate them to each other.

Direct Mail: By far, the most common method of building and maintaining a successful annual giving program is direct mail. This is because it has been proven to be effective and relatively inexpensive. I believe that the Internet will replace direct mail in the not too distant future because it will prove to be even more effective and inexpensive, but, until that day comes, a non-profit charitable organization needs to become very skilled at operating a mail program.

Purposes of Direct Mail

There are three purposes of a direct mail program: acquisition of new donors, renewing the gifts of those donors on a regular basis, and increasing the annual support from these donors. Only when we look at the three purposes together do we see the efficiency of this particular method. So that's how we will look at them first.

Generally speaking, a good acquisition letter to people who are not previous contributors produces about a 1% response, and the donations of that 1% of the people who responded usually cover the cost of the total mailing. In other words, for example, if you send an appealing acquisition letter to a 1,000 people, there is a good chance that about 10 of them will respond with a donation, and those 10 donations will probably cover the cost of the total mailing and not much more. So what's the point? The point is that we now have the potential to acquire 10 new regular donors. To carry the above example further, the next appeal letter to the 10 new donors will be much more targeted and personalized. And, if this is done effectively, chances are that 6 of them will respond with a new donation. These 6 donations will represent a real profit to the organization, given the fact that the only expense is the cost of mailing 10 letters. I have found that this second donation is key, because, if these newly acquired 6 donors are treated with care, it is very probable that they will stay with the organization as regular supporters for a very long time, and perhaps one of them will graduate one day into the ranks of the major givers to the charitable cause. When you multiply these numbers into the hundreds, thousands, and even millions, as is the case with some large organizations, it is easy to see how much of an impact a successful direct mail program can have on an organization's fundraising.

Lists of Names and Addresses

So how does a non-profit organization go about the development of a good direct mail program? Clearly the first step is to obtain a prospective list of names and addresses to which to send an appeal letter. This reminds me of a personal experience very early in my career when I knew almost nothing about fundraising. We recruited a group of volunteers to address envelopes to the residences listed in the telephone book of Cheyenne, Wyoming, a city of about 45,000 people at the time in which we had almost no current donors. We then enclosed an impersonal letter in each envelope and mailed the whole bunch. We did get a few responses, but not nearly the 1% mentioned above.

I laugh about this now. But I did learn a lot from the experience. And I use the experience to introduce the important point that we have to find ways to do better than the telephone book in obtaining lists of names and addresses for our acquisition mail program.

By far the most effective way is to gather together the names and addresses of those who have expressed some interest in your organization already. These are the people who call your office, attend your programs, receive your services, or have made some contact. In other words, these are people who know who you are and what you do, at least at some level. For example, during my career with the Arthritis Foundation, we established a regular program at our Chapter in which we sent a monthly fundraising appeal to all those who contacted our office by mail or phone for information, attended one of our educational programs, or participated in a service during that month. When we did this properly and in a timely way, we would produce a response rate of up to 6% at times, and always much better than the usual 1%. Thus, we were making a profit on these monthly mailings right away in addition to acquiring new donors for the future. Unfortunately, however, this most effective of methods is almost never enough to produce the numbers of regular donors we need. This is especially true for those organizations that do not have access to the huge numbers of people that the Arthritis Foundation does. So let's look at some other ways to do better than the telephone book.

A very common method among non-profit charitable organizations is to trade names and addresses with other similar organizations. For example, one health related organization may give names of donors to its organization to another health related group in exchange for a list of donors to that group. There are several advantages to this approach. There is no expense involved. The acquired list is composed of people who are interested in health issues. And these people have proven themselves to be responsive to fundraising appeals through the mail. But, despite these obvious benefits, I personally have never agreed with this practice of trading names. A recent study supports this opinion and is reported by Penelope Burke in her book as follows: "86% of individual donors will not knowingly support a charity that sells or trades their names with others." (1) Thus, most people appear to resent it when they learn that their names have been traded with other organizations. This makes it difficult to build a sense of loyalty among these donors. And, most of all, I think that there is much to gain from building a relationship of trust with our donors based upon a promise that, contrary to the wide practices within both the non-profit and for-profit business worlds, their names will not be shared with any other organizations. This gain in trust is worth more over the long haul than the economic savings and income that are gained from these trading practices. Nonetheless, I offer this method of acquiring names of prospective donors as an option in this text because it is a very common method and used successfully in many direct mail campaigns.

Another way to do better than the telephone book is to purchase lists of names of people that have demonstrated that they are "mail responsive" in many specific ways. There are lists made available through direct mail companies of people who are wealthy, who are seniors and wealthy, who are patriotic, who are motivated by their Christian beliefs, who are interested in children, who support animal welfare, who are devoted to the arts, and on and on. And purchasing such lists is not as expensive as you might think. Prices are usually below $100 per 1,000 names. You can also select names by zip code, so that you are sure that you are obtaining names in your service area or even in particular cities or neighborhoods. The names will come to you ready to use in mailing label format or almost any other format that you may need.

To conclude this section, most successful direct mail programs use a combination of the methods outlined above to constantly obtain the names and addresses they need to sustain this particular fundraising effort.

Direct Mail Design and Style of Letters

Now let's talk about the look and style of a direct mail communication. At a minimum, we want people to open and to read what we mail to them. A quick view of the many pieces of mail you receive every day, from both non-profit and for-profit sources, will indicate that all kinds of styles are being tried to achieve this objective. There is a vast array of colors, print types and sizes, and graphics being utilized. Most of these styles have been professionally tested on a small scale before they are reproduced and sent to thousands of addresses. So, as you are thinking about the design and style of the mailers you want to send out, consider what motivates you to open and read mail that you receive at the home or office. Like it or not, you are in competition with all of these different mailers for the attention and time of your prospects and donors.

Over the years, after much trial and error, we seemed to have the best luck with mailers that had the look and feel of a personal letter from our organization to an individual person or couple. The language used should be informal, like the way you would carry on a conversation, and free of jargon and esoteric words and phrases. And, contrary to the many long-winded fundraising letters I have seen over the years, I recommend that the letter be no more than one page. Give special attention to the opening sentence, the closing, the P.S., a graphic example or two of the difference your organization has made in people's lives, and a clear statement of why the generous support of **this** person is needed **now**.

There is a final, major point to be made about fundraising letters. An acquisition letter and a renewal letter should be very different in both style and content. An acquisition letter is written to **strangers** – at least relatively speaking – and you are trying to get their attention, to get them interested in supporting your charitable organization, and to tell them the difference they will make if they choose to make a contribution, even a very small one. A renewal letter is written to **friends**, and you already have their attention and interest. Remind them of the difference they already have made with their past support and thank them again for it. And oftentimes you may want to ask them to increase their donation over the previous amount, while pointing out the increased difference they can make if they do. Above all, to conclude this discussion, don't ever treat friends like strangers. That's the quickest way I know of to offend and to lose previous donors, even those who have supported your cause for a very long time.

Frequency of Renewal Letters

There appears to be quite a controversy in the field about how often to send fundraising renewal letters to previous donors. Direct mail experts have assumed for a long time that a high frequency – even almost every month – is effective. I have never agreed with this position. I have no doubts that such a frequent practice produces more donations and even more money in the short run. But I've always worried about the long run. I know for certain that many people – perhaps even most – are irritated by a high frequency of fundraising appeals. Again I quote from a recent study reported by Penelope Burke: "38% of individual donors will not give to a charity that sends duplicate or multiple solicitations; an additional 28% say it has an indirect, negative influence on their future giving decisions." (2) I think that this irritation over time causes us to lose donors that we may otherwise keep and to fail in upgrading the annual aggregate support of far too many of those we do keep. Besides, friends don't bug friends like this!

So what is a good frequency of renewal fundraising letters? My suggestion is two to three times per year. The first is to ask for the donor's annual gift (or membership renewal) and to give him or her reasons to increase that gift to as generous a level as possible. The second letter – an optional one – follows the first by two months or so and is sent **only** to those who have not responded to the first yet. It is a gentle reminder to a **friend**. The third letter is sent at a totally different time of the year to all on the entire previous donor list to request their special support for a particular program or aspect of your services. (In our case with the Arthritis Foundation, we made a special appeal for research funds.) No matter the specific reasons for your fundraising appeals, I suggest again that two or three times per year are enough. And remember that other communications with your regular donors **without** asking for money can and should be very frequent. These will definitely increase the number of responses and amounts resulting from your infrequent fundraising appeals.

In-House or Contracted Out

This is the final issue about direct mail fundraising. Should the non-profit organization implement this program itself with its own resources or contract it out to one of the many professional companies in this business in almost every moderate to major size city? This is not an easy question to answer. During my career, our Chapter of the Arthritis Foundation conducted its own renewal program and the smaller, manageable portion of our acquisition program (the monthly mailings to local contacts). However, because of economies of size, our acquisition program with large mailing lists was conducted by our National Office, which even contracted out some of the aspects of this to an outside company. My preference would be to do as much as possible in-house, which allows for a maximum amount of personalization. But, depending upon your particular financial goals, the numbers involved, and your own in-house technical competence, you may find it necessary, more economical, and more effective to contract out all or part of the operation. In any case, I would never stay very far away from the actual implementation of the direct mail program. This is particularly true in regard to the content of the letters involved and the frequency of those letters. You are making a huge positive or negative impression on the community by the quality of your direct mail program, especially if it reaches the size that it should be.

Telemarketing: Discussions about the other methods used in an annual giving program (namely telemarketing, the Internet, and person-to-person) will not be as extensive as the discussion just completed about direct mail, because many of the same principles already discussed apply as well to these other methods.

The first point to make about telemarketing is that it is decreasing in value and usefulness. This is primarily because of the increase of its perceived intrusiveness in the minds of people. It is also being replaced by other means of communication, especially the Internet. Nonetheless, it still has some significant value in an annual giving program of a non-profit charitable organization.

First of all, however, I would recommend against using telemarketing for donor acquisition. Given the fact that the organization has no real relationship with the prospects, we run the risk of causing more irritation than the very few positive responses may justify. It is a "cold call," as it is commonly understood to be, and it is difficult for both the prospect and the caller. But telephone calls can be used effectively in conjunction with direct mail to previous donors in two ways. The first option is to conclude an appeal letter – usually for a larger than normal contribution – with a sentence like: "I'll call you in a few days to talk further about this donation opportunity." Then the person will be expecting your call and it will not be perceived as an intrusion. Another good option is to call former donors who have not yet responded to the letter appeals for their renewal gift. We did this frequently during my career and found it to be most worthwhile. We were able to thank these people for their former support, learn about their reasons for giving, and obtain many renewal contributions that we may not have received otherwise. These were usually friendly conversations because we were calling people with whom we had established relationships, and they were not "cold calls" for either the donors or the callers.

The final issue to consider here is simply stated. Who should make the calls? There is no doubt in my mind that the most effective callers are people closely identified with the charitable organization, namely, its Staff, Board members, and volunteers. For example, the donor renewal calls referred to above were always done primarily by Board members and a few top level Staff members. When the phone call started with a statement like: "I am ___(Name)___, and I am on the Board of Directors (or on the Staff) of the Arthritis Foundation," the person usually responded very well to this introduction and oftentimes was truly impressed with the fact that someone that important in the organization was making the call. In fact, when I made these calls, donors often actually thanked me for taking the time to do so. This frequently happened with Board members and Staff as well.

I am sure that you have noticed that I have not included the option to have paid solicitors making the calls. Such calls are almost never received very well. The only positive exception in this regard may be when colleges pay current students a small amount to make phone calls to alumni about their annual contributions to their alma mater. The situation in this instance is enhanced for several reasons. There is a strong bond between the alumni and the college. Also alumni often actually enjoy talking with current students, and they appreciate the financially vulnerable position in which the students are. There may be other examples of a similar nature. But, generally speaking, I do not recommend the practice of hiring solicitors to make fundraising phone calls. It is unlikely that this can be really profitable over the long term, especially considering the very high fundraising costs that are usually involved.

Internet: There is no doubt that the Internet is a powerful, highly useful, fast, and economical means of communication between people and organizations. For several years now, it has been utilized in annual giving programs in non-profit charitable organizations, but, up until relatively recently, has not been very successful and was growing very slowly. But this all changed with the presidential campaign of Howard Dean just a few years ago. His success in raising funds through the Internet made a convincing argument that the Internet can be an effective tool. The Dean campaign workers collected the e-mail addresses of thousands of his supporters from throughout the country, and, at several critical junctures during the campaign, sent out urgent appeals for funds. The responses were overwhelming and almost immediate. Because of the astounding success achieved by the Dean campaign, the 2008 presidential campaign expanded the use of the Internet in political fundraising exponentially, as summarized in an article in TIME Magazine:

> For millions of Americans, the Internet has turned presidential politics into a fully interactive event, a chance to give money with mouse clicks and to volunteer virtually from miles away. And the Democrats have used these tools to produce historic results. In February alone Hillary Clinton was able to attract 200,000 new donors, most of them online, rescuing her campaign from the brink of bankruptcy. Obama has amassed an army of 750,000 supporters who have signed on to his website and participated in 30,000 offline events. Obama's online fund-raising eclipsed the $100 million mark in the first three months of the year, and his YouTube videos have been viewed 37 million times, a

figure that would make any television executive weep. (3)

This clear success of political fundraising over the Internet is now causing charitable organizations to expand their use of this method of fundraising exponentially as well. For example, a recent article in The Chronicle of Philanthropy summarized a survey on Internet use in non-profit fundraising. A total of 167 organizations reported that their donations over the Internet increased from about $366 million in 2004 to $908 million in 2005. One-third of the organizations stated that their on-line contributions more than doubled, and the rest reported increases of more than 50%. Some of the largest organizations in the survey provided evidence that fundraising over the Internet can account for 10% to 15% of the total amount of contributions given to these same organizations in a given year. (4) Such strong growth gives a clear indication that all charitable groups need to consider an expansion of their Internet activities. But how can they do so?

Obviously, the first step is to begin collecting e-mail addresses of their newly acquired and renewing donors, simply by asking for this information on donation forms. (I believe that this effort will be much more successful if assurance is provided that the addresses will not be shared with any other organizations.) Then I would launch some regular, short communications with those providing their e-mail addresses, updating them frequently on how their contributions are advancing the mission of the organization. In this process, you can advise them that you would like to start requesting their annual gifts over the Internet, pointing out the convenience for them and the cost savings for the organization. Provide every assurance that you will protect the credit and debit card information that will be necessary for these transactions. And then just try to renew some annual gifts in this manner, at least on a limited basis. The response rates and donation amounts will tell you quickly how successful this method is and who among your regular donors are comfortable with it. My judgment is that over time you will be able to convert more and more of your donors to using this methodology in their giving. Some will never change, of course. Their wishes will have to be respected.

Person-to-person: This last method to be discussed here and to be used in a charitable organization's annual giving program is the most effective one by far. When one person, ideally a donor volunteer and peer, personally asks another to make or renew an annual gift, the response is usually positive and more generous than those resulting from other methods. The problems with this method, however, are practical in nature. An annual giving program of any size at all would be extremely difficult to organize and implement in this way. But, given its effectiveness, I would try to use this methodology whenever possible and at least in a limited way.

As stated in the previous paragraph, the ideal person to make the ask has three characteristics. He or she is a donor, is a volunteer for the organization (A Board member is great!), and is a peer, associate, or friend of the person to be asked. Such a person has real leverage in the transaction and may prove to be indispensable in the annual gift renewal year after year. These points were brought home to me very emphatically some years ago. One of our Board members exercised regularly at a local athletic club because of her arthritis. While doing this, she made friends with a notable former athlete in the city. Because of their association, she was able to obtain a $1,000 annual gift from him. When it came time to renew that gift a year later, I asked the Board member if she would ask personally for the renewed contribution. She suggested that I draft a letter that she would sign. I did as she requested, and the letter was sent out from our office. A month went by and the donor did not respond. I told the Board member about this, and she agreed to talk with him the next time she saw him at the athletic club. He did not recall receiving a letter from her, but assured her that, if he did receive one, he would respond positively. What we concluded from all this was that I neglected to put her name as the sender on the return address of the envelope. Because I did not do this, he didn't even open the envelope. His donor relationship was through her – not directly with the Arthritis Foundation! Needless to say, we learned a good lesson. In future years, his renewal letter was always sent out with her name on the return address of the envelope. And we received a $1,000 contribution every time within only a few days.

I believe that this story illustrates two important points about the person-to-person approach to annual giving. It demonstrates clearly why this approach is so effective. It also illustrates why it would be extremely difficult to fully implement the method throughout a total annual giving program involving thousands of donors. There would be just too many details to manage effectively on an on-going basis. But, whenever it can be done, it should be done – and modern technology can be a tremendous help in this regard.

Before ending this discussion about the person-to-person approach in an annual giving program, I wish to mention a particular methodology that has been used successfully by many non-profit charitable organizations throughout the country. It is one developed by Terry Axelrod and carries the trademark of "Raising More Money." (5) The methodology involves including the person-to-person approach with a total organization effort to identify, inform, motivate, and finally ask prospects in a group to make an initial contribution, as well as renewed gifts on an on-going basis. I recommend it for your consideration.

Personalization and Promptness

I conclude this chapter on annual giving with a discussion about two characteristics of a successful program that are absolutely essential. The first is **personalization**. I am convinced that the more personalization we employ in our written, telephone, Internet, and person-to-person contacts, the greater will be our response rates and the more generous will be the contributions. This conviction flows from the facts that, when we are dealing with renewal donors, we are communicating with friends, and, when we are dealing with prospects, we are communicating with friends-to-be. Friends do not write letters to friends that begin with "Dear Friend" and that ignore the specific details of previous support. Let's look at two examples of a beginning of a letter to make this point clear:

Example #1:

Dear Friend:

We appreciate your past support. It made a real difference in many people's lives. Here is a story about one client who was helped because of your generosity.................

We hope that you will renew your support at this time – and even increase it if you can. If you do, it will help us to help even more people.

Example #2:

Dear Sally:

All of us here at the _____ (charitable organization) hope that you and your family are well and in good spirits. In particular, we hope that your new business venture continues to go well.

In behalf of our clients, we thank you again for your support

116

over the last three years. Those three $100 gifts made a real difference in the lives of the people we serve. Let me share a brief story about one of our clients who was helped because of your kindness................

I hope that you can renew your support at this time. Please consider increasing your gift to $125 – or even more – this time. Knowing you as I do, I am sure that you will increase your gift if you can. But, in any event, we and our clients will be thankful for whatever support you can send.

Obviously, the beginning of the first letter is impersonal and stiff, while that of the second one is personal and warm. The first one is re-produced easily, more quickly, and probably at much less cost, while the second demands more work, more time, and more cost. But I am certain that the percentage of positive responses and the total fundraising results will more than justify the increased work and cost. And the gap between the two approaches will only get larger as the years go by. The first approach runs the risk of at least lessening donor enthusiasm and oftentimes losing donor loyalty. The second approach has been proven to increase both donor enthusiasm and loyalty. Therefore, I strongly recommend that personalization be incorporated into your annual giving program in whatever ways that you can.

Now let me say a few words about incorporating **promptness** into your annual giving program. This is especially needed in the donor acknowledgement part of the program. During my career, I insisted that we acknowledge every contribution – no matter how small – as quickly as possible. When we were able to do this – either by mail or telephone – within 24 hours or so of the receipt of the gift, we made a positive and lasting impression on the donor.

When thinking about this, I suggest that you consider what goes through your mind when you personally make a contribution to a charitable organization. Your thoughts go something like this, if I can generalize from my own experiences. Did the organization receive my gift? Will it make a difference? If the organization answers these questions quickly, a positive impression is made with you. If it waits a while to do so – or never does – the opposite impression is made. And this positive or negative impression definitely affects your willingness to renew your support when given the opportunity in the future.

The interesting thing about promptness to my way of thinking is that it is a quality of the annual giving program that really costs nothing to implement. It is simply a habit to adopt throughout the charitable organization. Promptness in donor acknowledgement goes hand in hand with the courtesy extended in the total organization in returning telephone calls right away, responding quickly to postal and electronic correspondence, and simply being on time for appointments and meetings. If you are seen as a prompt and courteous organization, you will definitely stand out in the crowd and, without a doubt, enhance your fundraising success. And, again, it costs nothing to be prompt and courteous. It is a habit to instill in everyone, both staff and volunteers.

Bullet Summary

◆ The annual giving program in the charitable organization is the foundation of the total fundraising effort of the organization, and, through it, the organization reaches out to identify and solicit an ever-growing number of regular supporters.

◆ The first step in building an effective annual giving program in a non-profit charitable organization is to write a clear and compelling case for support, which becomes the foundation for all appeals to people for contributions.

◆ Based upon a yearly analysis of the fundraising results through the annual giving program, an organization needs to make efforts to replenish the natural attrition in the number of donors and actually increase the number of donors and amounts of contributions in order to keep up with inflation and to increase the services and outreach of the charitable organization.

◆ Direct mail is still the most common and efficient way to operate an annual giving program. To implement a mail program effectively, the charitable organization needs to continually add to its donor prospect list, obtain regular renewal gifts, and seek out increased support from those donors determined to be capable of it.

◆ Telemarketing works best when done by volunteers and in conjunction with the direct mail program.

◆ Use of the Internet in annual giving programs is increasing exponentially, largely because of its economies and flexibility. It will undoubtedly replace direct mail as the most common method in annual giving at some point in the not too distant future.

♦ A person-to-person approach in annual giving, although it is most often not practical to implement on a grand scale, is the most effective method and should be utilized as often as possible.

♦ Personalization and promptness are two essential characteristics of an annual giving program that will pay huge dividends in fundraising success.

Conclusion

Chapter 8 discussed the organization and methods of annual giving, which is the foundation of a comprehensive fundraising program in a non-profit charitable organization. It is the most important and usually the first program to be institutionalized in the organization, because all other methods of fundraising flow from the annual giving program and are dependent on it. The next chapter will talk about special events, which are common fundraising activities of many non-profit organizations and are done not only to raise funds, but also to raise public awareness and to introduce the organization to an additional group of potential on-going supporters.

(1) Penelope Burk, Donor Centered Fundraising, Cygnus Applied Research, Inc., Chicago, 2003, p. 21.

(2) Penelope Burk, Ibid. p. 22

(3) Michael Scherer and Jay Newton-Small, "Why Dems Rule the Web," TIME, April 28, 2008, p. 34

(4) Nicole Wallace, "Charities Make Faster Connections," The Chronicle of Philanthropy, January 15, 2006, pp. 19-25.

(5) Terry Axelrod, Raising More Money: A Step-by-Step Approach to Building Lifelong Donors," Raising More Money Publications, Seattle, WA, 2000.

Suggested Reading

Burk, op.cit., pp. 13-114.

Ciconte and Jacob, op.cit., 86-120

Chapter 9: But a Lot of People Came:

Special Events in Non-Profit Organizations

Many times in my career, after a special event in which the fundraising results were not very good, volunteers and staff, who had led the event, would report to the Board of Directors something like this: "We know that we did not reach our fundraising goals, but a lot of people came, and they said that they would come again next year if we hold the event again, because they had a good time." I was always disappointed when I heard such a report, because, as the Staff Executive of the organization, I was primarily looking for successful fundraising results from a great effort of a lot of people. But I had to acknowledge that some goals of the event were indeed realized because of the large participation, namely, an increase in public awareness and perhaps an identification of some new prospects for our annual giving program.

This frequent experience in the history of many non-profit charitable organizations points out a real problem in running special events. Oftentimes we fail to raise enough money to justify the volunteer and staff time and energy expended. I submit that the primary reason for these fundraising failures is the lack of proper planning for the events in the first place. Thus, we arrive at the major goal of this chapter. It is to help readers to understand how success in special event fundraising can only come from a thorough understanding of the nature of special events and the utilization of real discipline in the planning for them. With these thoughts in mind, the chapter will proceed as follows: First, I will explain why special events are very popular in non-profit organizations. Then, I will take a look at the wide range of such events in both variety and differing financial results. Third, I will point out the down side of special events, such as the volunteer and staff exhaustion that often results, and how this can be overcome. Then, I will discuss the importance of raising substantial dollars from sponsorships before the events are even held and the difficulties that sometimes arise in this pursuit. Fifth, I will add some strong advice about the specific planning that must be undertaken to assure financial success. Finally, I will conclude with some thoughts about how non-profit organizations can add to their regular list of contributors through their follow-up of the events.

The Popularity of Special Event Fundraising

There are many obvious reasons why special events are popular. These include the facts that they raise at least some money for charitable causes, they tend to increase public awareness, they may identify individual prospects for annual giving support, and they serve several social needs in the community. In speaking about serving social needs, I am talking about the needs for people to have fun in events like golf tournaments and runs, to give appropriate recognition to community leaders through award dinners and tribute events, to just "be seen" at high visibility social events, and to be entertained through film premiers and benefit performances. In general, many people enjoy the opportunity to have a good time and support charitable causes at the same time.

But there are other less obvious reasons for the popularity of special events. First of all, special events provide the opportunity for a large number of people, volunteers and staff who are otherwise involved with the charitable organizations, to work together in a spirit of teamwork to reach a common goal of raising dollars. The sense of togetherness and goal achievement reached in such events can pay huge dividends in carrying out the overall mission of the organizations through program activities. Secondly, many volunteers and staff may find it "easier" to be involved in fundraising through special events rather than through the "tougher" – at least in their view – methods of fundraising, such as actually asking someone for an outright contribution.

The challenge presented to volunteer and staff leaders of charitable organizations is to capitalize on the popularity of special events by bringing real discipline to their planning and implementation, so that they become a meaningful part of the total fundraising effort of the organization.

Variety in Types and Financial Results of Special Events

There is a huge range of special events, from the church bake sale that nets about $500, to the wine tasting and auction event that results in $25,000, to the award dinner that nets $100,000, and to the gigantic community race and walk that produces a net of about $1,000,000 or even more. For a long time, authors and leaders in the fundraising field insisted that special events were at most to be tolerated in the overall fundraising program of the charitable organization and ran the risk of being a distraction to real fundraising success. But many community events in recent years, notably the "Race for the Cure" done so well by the Komen Foundation for Breast Cancer Research, have proven them to be wrong. In Denver, for example, the "Race for the Cure" in recent years is an event with about 65,000 participants, and it nets over $3,000,000 in income. Thus, this annual event has become the cornerstone of the total fundraising program for the Komen Foundation.

Not every non-profit charitable organization can imitate the tremendous success of the Komen Foundation's "Race for the Cure." But every organization can exercise the required discipline in its planning and implementation of special events to make sure that significant fundraising results are attained and that they do not become a real distraction from the achievement of true fundraising success for the total organization.

The Downsides of Special Events

There are two downsides of special events that I have frequently witnessed in my career. The first is an extreme exhaustion among the volunteers and staff who are involved. The second is the seemingly never-ending amount of details that needs to be managed effectively throughout the process of conducting such events. Both of these are especially overwhelming to the development staff and volunteers, who have the overall responsibility for the total fundraising program. I suppose that there are many possible ways to overcome these downsides, but I will recommend one way that I have found to be effective.

What I tried to do in the later years of my career was to identify a few volunteers and a staff person (not necessarily from the development department) who were interested in and agreed to be a year round steering committee for each special event that we regularly conducted. Thus, when "their" event was completed for a given year, they immediately began advance preparations for the event to take place in the following year. They were able to gather suggestions for the improvement of the event, while it was fresh in everyone's mind, file these away, and use them as they began preparations for the next event. In other words, these small special event steering committees would think and talk throughout the year about how to make the event better and would be doing any necessary advance planning. Obviously, when the year moved ahead and the time for each event got into range, a larger committee was appointed to actually carry out the event. But the advance work of the small steering committees made the immediate preparations for each event go much more smoothly and with much less chance for the necessary details to be forgotten. I was never able to get this done for every special event, but, for those for which it was accomplished, there was a noted higher level of event implementation and fundraising success, and much less volunteer and staff exhaustion.

Raising Special Event Income from Sponsorships

As a general rule, much more money is actually raised from event sponsors than from the participants in the event itself. And this money must be obtained – or at least committed to – long before the event is held. (This, by the way, is another reason to have a year round event steering committee, as suggested above, because many sponsorships must be solicited several months before the event is scheduled.) But it is important to note that a high number of event participants is usually necessary for success in raising dollars from sponsors, especially if the sponsors are businesses as they tend to be, because they are seeking visibility among as many potential customers as possible.

Almost every special event lends itself to several levels of sponsorship. For example, fundraising dinners may have different table sponsorship levels with corresponding preferential seating. Or charity golf tournaments may "sell" eagle, birdie, and hole sponsorships for different amounts with corresponding benefits of participation and visibility for the respective levels. In addition, attempts should be made to have a title sponsor for each event. Such a sponsor becomes the "owner" or "presenter" of the event, and thus it becomes the "ABC Company Tennis Classic to benefit the XYZ Charity." This is the highest level of sponsorship and should be priced for at least double that of the other sponsorships. Businesses, in particular, understand these differentials in amount and visibility from their regular purchasing of advertising.

There are two important points to keep in mind when seeking sponsorships for special events. The first relates to the pricing of the various sponsorship levels. Far too many non-profit charitable organizations charge much too little for their sponsorships. We are often tapping into the advertising budgets of businesses when we seek their sponsorship support, and many businesses are used to spending a lot of money for exposure. If we can promise to provide – and actually do provide – a high level of exposure among people who are prime real or potential customers for their products or services, then we have every right to charge a corresponding amount for the visibility we give to businesses. (I will discuss what this might mean in actual dollars a bit later in this chapter.) The Komen "Race for the Cure" again presents a good example of this. Given this event's focus on women's health and the vast majority of participants who are women, many companies that promote women's health and sell women's products of all kinds are eager to be seen as sponsors at the "Race" each year and will pay a good amount for the opportunity. Also, many businesses just like to be associated with the worthwhile causes that we as non-profit organizations represent.

The other important point to make about sponsorships of our special events is the significance of affinity. In other words, we want to seek out sponsorships from those businesses that are related to the causes we represent or at least are not opposed to our missions. This is especially true because of the public nature of special events. For example, it would be clearly inappropriate for the American Cancer Society to accept a sponsorship from a tobacco company for one of its special events. In this discussion, I am reminded of a personal experience I once had in this regard. Our chapter of the Arthritis Foundation conducted a bed race event for a few years in which teams, composed of 4 runners and a rider in the bed that was put on wheels (the rider was usually a very light woman for obvious reasons) competed in a race. This spectacle of runners pushing beds down the street or track attracted a lot of spectators and organization visibility, but for some complex of reasons we were never very successful in raising any significant money from it. One year, a week before the bed race was to be held, I received a telephone call from the local theater that regularly showed XXX movies. The theater was eager to enter a bed in our race for a sponsorship fee, provided that we would permit one of its movie starlets to ride in the bed. We were assured that she would be appropriately clothed! I was proud of the response we finally gave to the offer after much thought. We turned the sponsorship offer down because arthritis seriously affects a disproportionate number of women over men, and we chose not to be identified with an industry that victim-izes women, at least in our opinion. I enjoy telling this story to my students when discussing this issue. Sometimes a student or two will argue against the decision we made, saying that perhaps we were being a bit prudish or old fashioned! But, none-theless, I believe that it presents a good illustration of the importance of appropriate affinity of sponsors of our special event fundraisers.

Effective Planning of Special Events

Now it is time to talk about the elements of an effective and disciplined planning process for special events. In my experience, I have found the following five rules to be especially helpful.

Rule # 1:   Focus the planning process on the bottom line: This is the most important rule of all. From the very beginning of the planning process, when the special event committee and its coordinating staff hold their first meeting, the Board Chair and/or Staff Executive need to make it very clear that the primary purpose of the special event is to raise dollars needed to support the mission of the non-profit charitable organization. I have seen too many committees get distracted from this primary purpose by getting caught up in the details of the event itself. In fact, I have often seen that this is all that some volunteers really want to do. They want to plan an enjoyable event for everyone and want nothing to do with raising money at all. If you find this to be the case with some volunteers on the committee, I would suggest to them that they form an event implementation sub-committee. Then they can focus on what they want to do, and the main planning committee can maintain its primary focus of raising money.

In thinking about this, I am reminded of a long-time volunteer leader who was a real asset in this regard. When he served on a special event committee and witnessed other volunteers getting caught up in the details if the event itself, he would imme-diately remind these volunteers that their purpose was to raise dollars, while others were responsible for the details of the event. Because he was a volunteer, he was much more effective in giving this message than a staff person could be. The Com-mittee Chair, being the volunteer leader of the event, is the ideal person to remind committee members about this and should be asked to do so.

There are probably many ways to keep special event committees and their staff members focused on the bottom line. One effective way is to use a "Special Event Worksheet," something like the one presented here as Figure 7, and to let it be a constant reminder to everyone about the primary purpose of the event. I recommend that it be used from the very beginning of the planning process until the actual event is held.

Figure 7
Special Event Worksheet

Name of Event:_____

Description of Event:_____

_____

_____

INCOME

One Title Sponsor @ $_____   =   _____

#_____ Other Sponsors @ $_____   =   _____

#_____ Participants @ $_____   =   _____

Other Income: _____   =   _____

TOTAL INCOME: _____

DIRECT EXPENSES

_____   =   _____

_____   =   _____

_____   =   _____

_____   =   _____

INDIRECT EXPENSES

_____   =   _____

_____   =   _____

_____   =   _____

_____   =   _____

TOTAL EXPENSES: =   _____

NET BENEFIT: =   **$50,000**

A worksheet, structured like this one with the financial goal or net benefit already filled in, will remind everyone involved from the very beginning and throughout the planning process that the primary purpose of the event is to raise a certain amount of money – in this case $50,000. Thus, all decisions made in the planning and implementation process can be focused on this bottom line. For example, as income is increased, the net benefit is increased. On the contrary, as expense is increased, the net benefit is decreased. And, equally as important, as expense is decreased – through obtaining donations of items that otherwise would have to be purchased as is often done – the net benefit is increased. If a worksheet like this one is frequently and effectively used by the event committee chair in particular, then real discipline and focus on the bottom line will guide the entire planning process. He or she can gently remind committee members and staff, especially when their discussions wander into less important areas as is often the case, that: "We are here to raise $50,000. Let's return our focus to this goal and make our decisions with it in mind."

I believe that almost all items on the worksheet presented as Figure 7 are clear except for the separate listing of "direct" and "indirect" expenses. Around this issue, we converge the financial management and fundraising parts of this text. **Direct expenses** are those associated with the implementation of the event itself. In other words, these are the costs related to the benefit that the participants receive. For example, the costs for the food, entertainment, logistics, fees, facilities, and arrangements are all listed under direct expenses. **Indirect expenses**, on the other hand, are those associated with the sponsor solicitation and promotion of the event. Thus, the costs for fundraising letters to potential sponsors, for advertising, and for the invitations to possible participants are all listed under indirect expenses. This distinction is important for financial management reasons, because the direct expenses are not really fundraising costs and, therefore, can be netted against the event income on the accounting records of the non-profit charitable organization. Indirect expenses, however, are fundraising costs and must be accounted for as such. So, as we try to keep our fundraising costs within reasonable bounds, the proper recording of these two kinds of expenses becomes very significant. **But** this distinction means nothing for the fundraising decisions being made during the planning and implementation of the event. Both direct and indirect expenses are included on the special event worksheet above and are netted against the income to determine the success or failure of the event. In this way we return to rule #1: Focus the planning process on the bottom line. Both direct and indirect expenses must be kept within reason if the fundraising goal or net benefit is to be achieved.

Perhaps it might be helpful now to complete the Special Event Worksheet above with these thoughts in mind for a wine tasting special event. The exact numbers and names are fictional, but they are based upon real events of this nature with which I have had much experience.

Figure 8
Special Event Worksheet

Name of Event: <u>Western Wine Distributors Fourth Annual Wine Tasting Event to Benefit the Flower City Community Foundation</u>

Description of Event: <u>Over 100 kinds of wine, provided and poured by 20 different wine distributor companies, are sampled by participants. In addition, six restaurants provide snack foods, and there is a silent auction.</u>

INCOME

One	Title Sponsor	@ $10,000	=	$ 10,000
# 20	Table Sponsors	@ $500	=	$ 10,000
# 500	Participants	@ $50	=	$ 25,000
Silent Auction:		$15,000	=	$ 15,000
TOTAL INCOME:			=	**$ 60,000**

DIRECT EXPENSES

Rental of Hotel Ballroom	=	$ 1,500
Hotel Service, Equipment, and Table Set-ups	=	$ 1,000
Musical Entertainment	=	$ 500
Security and Special Event Insurance	=	$ 1,500
Commemorative Wine Glasses	=	$ 2,000
Program Printing	=	$ 500

INDIRECT EXPENSES

Printing of Invitations and Posters	=	$ 1,500
Advertising	=	$ 1,000
Postage	=	$ 500
	=	
TOTAL EXPENSES:	=	**$ 10,000**
NET BENEFIT:	=	**$ 50,000**

Clearly one of the primary reasons for the financial success of this special event is the fact that all the wine, food, and auction items provided for the participants at the wine tasting are donated. And, considering that the solicitation of these items is done by the volunteers on the event planning committee, the net benefit is increased even more. Both of these accomplishments can be done – and I have actually seen it being done several times – but not without a lot of skilled organizational work on the part of the staff and the effective leadership of the committee chair.

Rule #2: Don't have the event if you cannot reach an acceptable level of fundraising success. This is sometimes a most difficult rule to follow, especially because volunteers and staff working on special event committees tend to become highly invested in the events for which they are planning. With this in mind, it needs to be made very clear in the very beginning of the planning process, again ideally by the Chair of the Board and/or the Staff Executive, that the event is to be cancelled or postponed if an acceptable level of fundraising success cannot be envisioned. For example, the $50,000 net goal cited above in Figure 7 may be ideal and strived for. Perhaps, in this context, $30,000 is determined to be a minimum expectation. Thus, if after the event committee works and re-works the special event worksheet, a net result of at least $30,000 cannot be almost guaranteed, then the very difficult decision has to be made – hopefully by the event committee itself because it fully understands the administrative directive already given – to forego the event, at least for now. Of course, what we really hope to achieve by rule #2 is a successful special event because those involved are driven by the bottom line and fully understand the primary reason for the event in the first place.

Rule #3: Strive to achieve a level of sponsorship income that at least covers the total cost of the special event. Observance of this rule is a way to make sure that a profit will be made in the implementation of the event, resulting from 100% of the fees charged to participants. It also gives a clear and specific minimum goal for the event committee and its staff for sponsorship income. Of course, we should plan and hope for a higher level of such income. But even this minimum level will not be achieved unless those involved fully understand the point made earlier in this chapter, namely that sponsorships must be priced at adequate dollar amounts. We are selling a real value to potential sponsors, and we should not diminish that value by charging too little for it.

Rule #4: Charge adequate amounts to participants in special events: I have often seen in my career that this rule is very difficult for many non-profit charitable organizations to observe. They frequently get caught up in the desire to make sure that a good crowd will be in attendance or even forget the primary purpose – raising money – of what they are doing. As a result, they are concerned about charging too much. I am reminded about an experience I had in a community in Montana several years ago. After a lot of work, I convinced our volunteer group there that it could have a fundraising dinner honoring a respected physician in its town. Our local staff person even recruited the doctor for the event and found that he was excited about this possibility to use his community recognition to raise dollars for the mission of the Arthritis Foundation. Then I learned that the volunteer group had decided to charge $25 per person for the dinner – barely covering our coats – to assure that there would be a large attendance to honor the physician. One volunteer even re-marked that, if she were Dr. _____, she would be disappointed to learn that we were actually trying to make money through the event! After much argument and convincing our local group that the physician would be displeased if money was not raised for our mission, the group reluctantly agreed to charge $50 per person. As a result, we held a reasonably successful award dinner event that netted a few dollars for the cause.

But what is an adequate amount to charge? My recommendation is to charge at least double the market value of what the participants actually receive. So, if the dinner value – as in the example above – is $25, then we should charge $50. If our costs per golfer in a golf event are $100, then we should charge $200. This allows us to tell participants that half of their fee is tax deductible. But there is another consideration. We should research the community to find out what other charitable organizations are charging for similar events. This assessment of the "market" may lead us to charge more or less. But, if it is less, we should never reduce it so much that a real donation to a charitable cause is not involved. After all, we are not show-ing people a good time for that reason alone. Restaurants and golf courses do that. We are involved in this kind of fundraising to promote our very important missions – and that is our only reason.

Rule #5: Choose an appropriate target group for each special event. As men-tioned previously in this chapter, fundraising success in special events is determined largely by the number and characteristics of the participants in the events. This is even true for sponsorship income, because potential sponsors assess this factor when they make their funding decisions. As a result, especially when we are planning a new event, we need to force ourselves to think long and hard about what groups of people will be attracted to participate. Mistakes in this regard can be very costly.

I am reminded about a most successful special event conducted by the Multiple

Sclerosis Society. It was not at all successful in the beginning, however. The "MS 150" is a bike ride of 150 miles over a two-day weekend. As I understand it, the initial target group for the event was composed of members of bike clubs. However, this group produced very few participants, largely because the bike club members were very used to riding 150 miles on a weekend and, as a result, were not at all challenged to participate in the event. Once this was learned through trial and error, the MS Society began to promote the event among less regular bike riders, among those who would find 150 miles to be a real challenge. Only in this way did the "MS 150" become a huge success, netting very significant dollars for the mission of the MS Society.

The lesson here is clear. A "build it and they will come" mentality just doesn't work with special events. There is a lot of competition out there when it comes to special events. There is a premium on creativity, quality, and plain old market research. Choose your target groups for your special events with great care and find effective ways to encourage their participation. Only then will our special events become the "thing to do" for a lot of people, and only then will they achieve their fundraising goals.

Special Events and Annual Giving

Non-profit charitable organizations can maximize their hard work in putting on special events by identifying new prospects for their annual giving programs from among the participants in those events. A good special event will attract many people who have no previous allegiance to the mission of your organization. And, among those people, are some who, with a bit of encouragement, could become regular contributors.

As I think about this, I am reminded about a wine tasting event that we conducted for several years. It was a moderately successful fundraiser, reaching an approximate net benefit of $40,000 at its height. But what was especially exciting to me was the fact that, as I walked around the room, I would only know and be able to recognize about 10% of the 500 or so attendees. Most of the rest of the people were not there primarily because they wanted to support our cause. They were there to taste over 100 kinds of wine! I was enthused about this because, given the high incidence of arthritis, there was a good chance that many of them had some interest in our mission and would become regular supporters if we could identify and solicit them effectively.

With these thoughts in mind, I recommend that non-profit organizations should go through these steps after each special event. First, review the list of attendees and identify those who are already regular contributors and those who are not. Then, write a letter to the first group, thanking them for their participation, asking for their suggestions for improving the event, and, above all, taking the opportunity to thank them again for their regular support. Finally, I would craft and send a letter something like this to those who are not regular contributors:

Dear _____ :

I noticed that you were in attendance at our _____ event last Friday evening. I hope that you enjoyed the event. We worked hard to make it enjoyable for everyone. We plan to hold the event again next year about this time. If you have any suggestions on how the event could have been made more enjoyable for you and others, please let us know by sending them to us in the enclosed envelope.

Thank you very much for your participation. Your support, joined with that of everyone else who was there, resulted in a net benefit of $_____ for the charitable work of the _____ organization. As a result, we will be able to expand our services so intensely needed by our clients. They join us in expressing deep gratitude to you.

As you may know, our mission is to _____ _____ _____. I hope that you are someone who has some interest in this mission and would consider becoming a regular contributor to our work. If you are, please complete the contact information on the enclosed form and send it to us in the return envelope. We will then send you an information packet on what we do and why for you to review.

Thank you again for your participation. You have already made a huge difference in the lives of many people.

Most sincerely,

_____

Notice in the letter that a contribution is not asked for at this time. As stated previously in this text, every thank you letter should stand alone as an expression of gratitude, without soliciting another donation. But, if someone takes the time to respond to this letter, it is very likely that he or she will become a contributor with a positive response to the information packet, which contains a solicitation, or later on in response to your annual appeal.

If a non-profit organization follows-up its special events in a similar way, the fundraising results of these events will definitely increase. And be sure to advise your volunteers and staff, who have worked so hard to put on the events, of this added result of their exceptional efforts.

Bullet Summary

♦ Oftentimes non-profit charitable organizations fail to raise enough money through their special events to justify the time and expense involved. This is largely due to a lack of disciplined planning in implementing these events.

♦ Nonetheless, special events are very popular in non-profit organizations, largely because they serve several purposes.

♦ There is a huge variety in special events, both in kinds and in fundraising results achieved. Contrary to professional opinion for many years, these events can and do raise very significant dollars for charitable causes.

♦ Downsides of special event fundraising are staff and volunteer exhaustion and the effort needed to effectively manage the seemingly never-ending details involved. Both of these can be mitigated, however.

♦ Generally speaking, more funds are raised in special events from sponsorships than from participants. But this requires adequate pricing and selecting sponsors with a real affinity to the organization's mission.

♦ Effective planning and implementation of special events is greatly enhanced through the observance of five rules:

    1. Focus constantly on the bottom line.

2. Be willing to postpone or cancel an event if financial success is not assured.

3. Attempt to have sponsorship income cover at least the costs of the event.

4. Whenever possible, participant fees for special events should be set at twice the market value received.

5. Special care needs to be given to the choice of target groups for special events.

◆ Non-profit charitable organizations should thank the attendees in their special events afterwards for their participation, making specific efforts to identify those who may become regular contributors to their annual giving programs.

Conclusion

Chapter 9 gave a broad overview of special events as potential fundraisers for non-profit charitable organizations, as well as serving many other purposes both for the organizations and for society. The key message here is that special events need effective, disciplined planning to be successful in their primary purpose – the raising of significant funds to support charitable causes. Now, in Chapter 10, we move on to a natural outgrowth of the constituent building fundraising programs discussed so far, namely to major gift fundraising. Here we will focus on raising very significant dollars from relatively few people.

Suggested Reading

Ciconte and Jacob, op.cit., pp. 225-252.

Chapter 10: **They Let Me Put Our Names on a Building:**

Major Gifts in Non-Profit Organizations

Early in my years with the Arthritis Foundation, I did something out of ignorance and inexperience that, up to this day, is the worst fundraising mistake I ever made throughout my professional career. There were a husband and wife who, in response to the annual solicitation for their membership renewal, would send in an exceptional contribution of $1,000. This went on for several years, even after the husband had died. I always sent them – and later on her – a personally written thank-you letter, because, at this time in our history, gifts of this size were very rare. But I made no effort to get to know them better or even to call them on the telephone. Then the annual contributions stopped. After noticing this for two years, I gathered up some nerve and called her on the telephone. When I told her who was calling, she responded with obvious coolness. So I nervously thanked her for her past contributions and mentioned that we had missed them over the past two years. She immediately responded that she had lost interest in our cause. When I asked if she perhaps might renew her interest and support (I knew that she had arthritis), she replied in the negative and said that she now was interested in something else. I then asked her what she was now interested in, and she responded with the name of a local university. She even went on to tell me why in these words: "They let me put our names on a building." Our conversation then ended because I really didn't know what else to say. She never did renew her support.

A few years later I heard about a new building that was now finished at the local university. It was being dedicated to the same husband and wife, who had made a multi-million dollar gift! I learned an important lesson through this mistake. An organization should never take generous annual gifts for granted and should follow-up on them with something more than a personal letter. And, if I knew then what I know now about major gift fundraising, I may have been successful in encouraging these people to make a very large gift to the Arthritis Foundation.

This experience, drawn from my early executive career, not only illustrates my own lack of knowledge about major gift fundraising at that point in my professional life. It also illustrates the wider fact that the concept of major gift fundraising was almost totally foreign to the thinking of voluntary health and human service organizations in this country until about 10 or 15 years ago. Such fundraising has long been a mainstay for institutional development programs in hospitals, universities, and other large non-profit organizations. But only in relatively recent years has this very efficient method to raise large amounts of contributed dollars been implemented in the smaller, community based non-profit organizations. However, we still have a long way to go. The primary goal of this chapter is to demonstrate that the tried and true principles of major gift fundraising, even if they are implemented only in a limited way, can have a tremendous positive impact on the financial support of smaller, charitable non-profit organizations in almost any field of endeavor.

With this final thought in mind, I will first introduce you to the concept of major gift fundraising. Then, I will point out the necessity for overall coordination of the major gift program. Third, we will go through at length the six steps in the major gift fundraising process. I will conclude with a discussion about donor recognition – a most important component of a successful major gift program.

Introduction to Major Gift Fundraising

Major gift fundraising is a natural outgrowth of the fundraising programs talked about previously, specifically annual giving and special events, through which relatively small contributions are sought from an ever-growing number of people. It is an outgrowth of those fundraising efforts because, among the numerous donors who make annual gifts and support special events, there are some who would consider making truly substantial gifts to the non-profit organization with appropriate encouragement. The challenge, of course, is to identify these potential major donors and to cultivate them with skill and sensitivity.

But what is a major gift? The answer to this question depends upon the size, culture, and particular needs of each organization. Some charitable groups may consider a gift of $250 or $500 to be a major gift. While other more established and larger institutions may not consider a gift to be major until it reaches the level of $1 million or more. The amount doesn't really matter. A major gift of any size almost always requires that a definitive process be undertaken – a process in which the particular donor is appropriately identified, cultivated, and finally asked to make a major gift.

And this process often takes a long time, usually six months to up to two years. For this reason, a non-profit organization cannot expect to have instant results when it decides to employ this method of fundraising.

Let's talk more about the process of major gift fundraising. I have seen over the years many descriptions of the major gift fundraising process, but the one that proved to be most useful to me is the one proposed by Jerold Panas, who is a development professional and consultant of the highest order. I have benefited immensely from his writing and his seminars. In his book, entitled <u>Finders Keepers,</u> Jerold delineates six steps in the major gift process in the format of "I,s" as follows:

1. **Identify** the potential major donor.

2. **Interest** that person in the work of your organization.

3. **Involve** the prospect in your work.

4. **Intervene** meaningfully in the life of the person.

5. Ask the person to **Invest** significantly in your organization.

6. Finally, suggest that the donor use his or her **Influence** to encourage others to make similar gifts. (1)

Thus, the major gift process is logical and progressive in nature. The charitable organization runs the risk of making a severe mistake leading to under-performance or even failure if it either hurries through the process or omits some of the steps along the way. The process is also cyclical in two ways. First, the major donor prospect may be taken back through the process again and again in pursuit of additional major gifts, and, second, the 6th step of "influence" often leads to the beginning of a totally new process with someone recommended by the major donor.

A good friend, who worked as a development professional at a local university for several years, first introduced me to this process of major gift fundraising. His total responsibility was to continually take 100 major donor prospects through the six "I's" described above. Specifically, he tried to acquire an annual gift from each of his "clients" – as he described them – each year and, from time to time – perhaps at 5-year intervals – ask them for a major gift to the university, usually for a very specific project. What impressed me the most about his implementation of the the

6-step process was the fact that he became a close friend of his donors as he intervened in their lives and involved them in university activities and events in many different ways. He exemplified for me over and over again the conceptual approach to fundraising defined in Chapter 7 as a voluntary exchange among people.

Coordination of the Major Gift Program

This discussion about my friend in university development leads us to an important issue: Who should coordinate the major gift program? In my friend's case, he was the official coordinator for "his" prospects and donors. He was the one who knew where each of his clients were in the six "I's" at any given moment and was in charge of orchestrating the university's communication with each one. Whenever anyone else wished to communicate with one of his clients, he or she would first contact my friend for advice before proceeding. Everyone else knew that it was his full-time job to maintain and cultivate the relationships with his prospects. But not many non-profit charitable organizations, especially in their first efforts at major gift fundraising, can afford to hire or assign a single individual to work in this area. However, every organization can incorporate this concept of coordination in regard to each major donor prospect. In other words, one person needs to be designated to be the official coordinator of the six "I's" with each individual prospect. All communication of the organization with each prospect does not necessarily need to go through the coordinator, but he or she needs to know about it and be given the opportunity to offer appropriate advice. Additionally, in some instances, the coordinator may actually invite others, staff or volunteers, to communicate with the prospect when appropriate or needed around certain matters.

So how best might this be done, especially in the beginning when no one person is assigned exclusively to the major gift program? When we began to concentrate on major gifts, we identified about 80 prospects. Of these, we assigned 40 to me as the Staff Executive, 20 to the Development Director, and 20 to our Operations Director. The three of us often conversed about our progress with our prospects, but each of us knew very well about who had the individual responsibility for each prospect. This seemed to work quite well. Thus, this is one option. Another might be to assign only one staff person to the coordination responsibility in the beginning, especially if the prospect numbers are smaller. But I believe strongly that the Staff Executive needs to be heavily involved in every phase of this program, ideally as an actual coordinator.

The Six Steps of the Major Gifts Process

Now I will use six steps of the major gifts fundraising process, as suggested by Jerold Panas, as a guide in a discussion on how this process can best be implemented in the non-profit charitable organization.

Step One: Identify: In the identification phase of the major gifts process, we are looking for people, either from among our current supporters or elsewhere, who may have the capacity and willingness to make a substantial contribution to our organization. This is a most important phase of the process as exemplified by the hospitals, universities, and other large institutions that have been in the major gift fundraising business for a very long time. They have whole departments, or at least a few individuals, doing nothing but "prospect research," as it is called in the language of these institutions. The professionals involved spend their entire workdays gathering and recording information about current and prospective donors to their institutions. They build and maintain lengthy files on each prospect, treat the information contained in absolute confidence, and only share the information with the institutions' fundraising professionals and administration on an as needed basis. They also maintain summaries of all contacts made by institutional representatives with the prospects.

Some of my graduate students are frequently quite disturbed when we discuss this topic of prospect research. They feel that we are talking here about real invasion of privacy. I usually respond to their concerns in several different ways:

> a. Most of the information gathered while doing prospect research is in the public domain already. The business and society pages of the daily newspaper are full of information on people, on their work, and on their interests. The Internet, especially through search programs like Google, is also a tremendous resource for data about people. The researcher simply gathers and records such publicly available information that may be useful to the fundraising program.

> b. Much of the information gathered is actually provided by the people involved. Examples of this are the personal data contained in publications like "Who's Who in America" and the social registries published in almost every larger-than-average city in the United States. People choose to be listed in such publications,

provide the actual information about themselves, and oftentimes even pay for the perceived privilege. So gathering such personal data is hardly an invasion of privacy.

c. Information gathered through prospect research should be – and usually is – treated with professionalism and confidentiality and shared only on a real need-to-know basis. In fact, the professional association of prospect researchers in the fundraising business has a code of ethics that demands such treatment of personal information.

d. The final point I usually make is based upon the concept that fundraising – especially major gift fundraising – is a "voluntary exchange among people." Therefore, both the volunteer and professional fundraiser need to know if there is a match between the needs of the non-profit charitable organization and those of the prospective donor. Definitive conclusions about such a match are only reached through communications back and forth between the donor and the organization's representatives, but good prospect research can lead to preliminary conclusions about this important consideration and thus minimize the chance of wasted effort and disappointment.

Now how does the relatively average or small non-profit organization, one which has no prospect research department or a research professional on staff – which, I believe, is the case for the vast majority of charitable organizations – go about identifying prospects for its major gift program? One way is to simply go through the annual giving records of the organization and to select out those who are already giving at a higher than average level – $250 and above, for example. This is how we identified the initial 80 prospects for our major gift program that I spoke of above. In this regard, we made the assumption that donors at this level had greater than average capacity and interest to make even larger contributions. This assumption proved to be true in many instances.

Another way is to organize a rating group. To do this, you select 7 to 10 people from among your Board of Directors and volunteers who are relatively connected in the community and seem to know a lot of people. Then, in a confidential meeting setting, you present these people with a list, for example, of 100 local donors who are now making annual gifts of $100 or more. Then you ask them to talk about any on the list that they know, especially in regard to their interest in the organization and their capacity to make larger contributions. You may also ask such a group if it knows of others, perhaps not on your organization's donor list, who may have similar interest and capacity. Over the years, I have been amazed at how much certain Board members and other volunteers know about other people and how willingly they will share this information when asked, especially when they know that the information will be treated with confidence and only be used for the mission of the organization.

A final way I wish to suggest to identify prospects for a beginning major gifts program is to pay for the services of the many data gathering companies organizations that exist. You can share a list of donors with such an organization and ask it to run your list against the huge database it has. It will then give you back a wealth rating on each donor. There are also computer software programs that do the same. These approaches can be relatively costly, especially in contrast to the research options above, but, if the other methods do not produce enough prospects for your organization's fundraising goals, the investment may be very well worth it.

In any event and as long as you now have identified even a few real prospects for your major giving program, you can proceed ahead to the next step with the prospects you have. And I strongly recommend that you go forward with only the number of prospects that you can manage well within the human and financial resources of your non-profit charitable organization.

Step Two: Interest: This step in the major gift process begins with an assessment of the level of interest of the individual prospect and of the reasons for that interest in your non-profit charitable organization. To my way of thinking, there is only one way to make this assessment, and that is through real communication with the prospect, preferably face-to-face or at least over the telephone. Once polite greetings are exchanged, the conversation can go something like this: "Thank you for your generous support of our work that, according to our records, now extends back to over _____ years. Because of that support, I assume that the work of our organization must be important to you. Is that true?......... Could you share with me the **specific reasons why** you do support our charitable work?" The answer to this last question is the key to all that follows in the major gift process. The answer should be referenced in all future communications with the prospect and most probably will be the basis for the "invest" or "ask" step in the process when that moment is finally reached.

In Chapter 7 we already talked about the importance of knowing the specific motivation that guides an individual's giving. Perhaps an example here might strengthen this point. I remember getting to know an elderly gentleman who all of a sudden began to make $250 annual contributions to the Arthritis Foundation. I arranged to visit him in his home, which was in a large senior citizen complex. When I asked him a question something like the one above, he explained that his wife, who had suffered with rheumatoid arthritis for many years, died a couple of years before. He missed her terribly and was obviously lonely without her. His generous gifts to the Foundation were a way to honor and remember her. Once I knew this important piece of information, I referred to it whenever I visited with him in the future, either over the telephone or in person over lunch and when I wrote an annual appeal letter and subsequent thank-you letter to him. We were able to build a real friendship around this single point. Unfortunately, this elderly gentleman became quite ill himself after a couple of years and died. As a result, I was never able to reach the "invest" stage with him. But you can be sure that, if we did, we would have talked about further ways to honor his late wife.

As we discuss the motivation for charitable giving, I am reminded about the fact that over the years many professional associates and students exaggerate the importance of tax deductions in major gift fundraising. Personally, I have never found that such deductions from personal income tax are ever the primary reason for generous charitable contributions. There is always some other meaningful reason for the gift in the first place. What I have found, however, is that the personal tax deduction is often a reason for an increased gift. I learned this from a most generous major donor several years ago. This particular gentleman made an annual gift of about $15,000 per year, and he made it clear that his primary reason for giving was his wife, who was severely debilitated with arthritis for a very long time. His usual method of giving was in the form of a stock certificate, but the time of year in which he would make his gift was never predictable. But he would always make his gift by personally delivering the stock certificate to me in my office. On one of these occasions, I gathered up enough nerve to ask him why he chose to make his gift in this way. He willingly explained that, several years ago, he had purchased the stock certificate for about $5,000. Now it had increased in value to $15,000. If he had sold the certificate, he would be liable for capital gains tax on the $10,000 profit. But, because he gave the certificate to the Arthritis Foundation, he not only avoided the capital gains tax, but he also benefited from a tax deduction on the whole amount of $15,000. What pleased him was the fact that, for his original cost of $5,000, he was able to make a $15,000 charitable gift to benefit his wife and others like her, which was his annual goal.

The secondary importance of tax deductions in charitable giving was verified in a recent survey of wealthy donors commissioned by the Bank of America and reported over the Internet by The Chronicle of Philanthropy. (2) The survey interviewed "945 households in neighborhoods across the country where the average household had liquid assets of at least $3-million." Almost 100% of the households responded that they had made a charitable gift during the last year. "Respondents cited meeting critical needs, giving back to society, and helping those less fortunate as top motivations for making charitable gifts. If no tax advantages could be reaped from donations, about half of the survey respondents said there would be no change in their giving and only 7 percent said donations would 'dramatically decrease.'" The report went on to say that "People are going to use some of the tax advantages in giving but they are not necessarily using the taxes as the prime driver of why they give." I would add that tax advantages are almost never the "prime driver" in charitable giving – at least in my experience. Regardless of the tax benefits, any charitable gift is still going to cost the donor something.

The point of this discussion is that there is almost always some deep, heartfelt reason why an individual person makes a gift to a charitable cause. During this step in the major gift process, the volunteer or professional fundraiser needs to find out what this reason is. This issue becomes even more important when it is time to explore the reasons why an individual donor may be motivated to make a much larger contribution. This is usually a much more difficult conversation to have. For this reason, it may be best to delay this exploration until the process has advanced into further steps. But the fundraiser should be looking for clues to this potential motivation during the "Interest" step and later on as the donor prospect is further informed about the work of the organization and actually becomes involved in it.

Step Three: Involve: Once the coordinator of the process is satisfied that an individual donor prospect has a real interest in the work of the non-profit charitable organization and is convinced that this interest can grow, it is time to move on to the involvement stage. I believe that this step is the most important of all, except of course for the invest step. The challenge here is to find ways to actually involve the person in the work of the organization, so much so that the person begins to think and to say that this is "my organization." There are several possible ways to go about this, and the best way that I can explain them is to use actual examples from my experience.

A good preliminary way is to invite the donor prospect to attend an educational session on the organization along with other interested people, to be present and introduced at a meeting of the Board of Directors, to witness an actual program of the organization, and to meet significant volunteer leaders and staff of the organization. I found, for example, that our Board meetings were interesting to a guest because they usually had an educational component to them, and the Board members themselves were enthusiastic about the organization and expressed this often in their discussions. Depending on the particular interest of the donor prospects, I would take them to an arthritis research laboratory at the local medical center and allow them to meet and converse with someone actually engaged in arthritis research or invite them to visit our camp for children with arthritis. These proved to be powerful ways to involve them in our work, at least in a preliminary way. And, in general, I have discovered that introductions to others, who are already highly motivated and already deeply involved in our work, are also very powerful.

A deeper and perhaps more subtle way to involve a donor prospect in the work of the organization is to seek his or her advice on how a program or activity of the organization can be improved. I often tell my students – and they readily agree – that asking someone for his or her advice is a wonderful way to compliment a person. And, in the context of major gift fundraising, I know of no quicker way for a donor to feel that he or she is now a real participant in the work of the organization.

As I write about this, I am reminded of a regular major donor of $5,000 to $10,000 per year to the Arthritis Foundation. She was already a member of our Board of Directors and was always positive and supportive at meetings of the Board. But, once a year around the time for her to make her annual gift, we would go to lunch and she would complain vehemently about some activities of our Chapter that needed to be improved in her mind. When I would ask her how this might be accomplished, she was always full of good ideas. Invariably, when I drove her home from lunch, she would invite me into her home where she would write and present to me her very generous donation check. I know that she felt very involved in our work, especially because I, as the Staff Leader of the Chapter, took the time to really hear her suggestions and chose to implement many of them.

Over the years, after taking some of the preliminary steps discussed above, I would often invite some of the donor prospects to actually serve on the Board of Directors or one of our committees. If this invitation is accepted, this represents the ultimate in involvement. Of course, not everyone is ready or even interested in such a large responsibility. But, for those who are, this gives a strong indication to the charitable organization that the person is willing and perhaps even ready to make a major gift.

<u>Step Four: Intervene</u>: In this step, the non-profit charitable organization, usually through its coordinator and other significant volunteer and staff leaders, regularly makes meaningful interventions into the lives of its major donor prospects. This can be as simple as recognition of birthdays, holidays, or other celebratory events in their lives. Or, on the other hand, it may involve giving support in times of illness or other difficult times. I believe that it is important to stress that such interventions need to be **meaningful**, as mentioned above in this paragraph. Anyone can easily see through a perfunctory or insincere contact.

Let me give some of examples of what I mean by a meaningful intervention. I have a vivid memory of a visit I made to a regular generous donor couple in a relatively small Colorado town. I knew the wife quite well, but had never met the husband. She arranged for us to meet in the office of their family business, a steel company run by her husband. As I entered the room that day, I could tell immediately that her husband was not at all pleased to be in such a meeting. I quickly explained that I was there to just say thanks for their generosity over the years and to talk about what their gifts had enabled us to do for people with arthritis. The wife and I carried on a conversation for a while, but it was very difficult to include her husband. I finally decided to follow a piece of advice given to me by my late father many years ago, which was to ask people what they do when you want to carry on a good conversation. So I asked the husband what he did there at the steel company. He became animated right away and went into a long description of what their company was all about – so long that his wife excused herself to go to another appointment. I left the steel company an hour later, after a full tour wearing a hard hat and meeting every one of his employees. I learned just a short time ago that the Chapter is still receiving major annual gifts from the wife (the husband having died a few years ago), but now these gifts are often doubled to the level of $10,000 per year. I am confident that this continued giving has something to do with the meaningful intervention I made.

Supporting people in their times of difficulty and sorrow can also be a meaningful intervention. I would often visit people when they were in the hospital and attend their family funerals. You may object and say that this is a job for a member of the clergy. But if these donor prospects are now truly involved in the organization, if they are now members of the group's family, then such interventions come across as sincere and most appropriate.

I learned a lot about making meaningful interventions in the lives of donor prospects from my friend working in university development that I spoke about earlier in this chapter. The university gave him a relatively large personal budget to do such things as hosting his prospects on the fifty-yard line at university football games and taking them out to dinner on special occasions. But I also remember him attending an Arthritis Foundation fundraising dinner once. When I asked him why he was there, because I knew that he had no personal reason to support the arthritis cause, he said simply that he was there because 4 or 5 of his prospects were there. He just wanted to meet and visit them in a setting that was meaningful to them.

When I have talked with volunteers, my staff, and my students over the years about this step in major gift fundraising, I am often asked what should they talk about so that they can come across as sincere and thoughtful. I often respond to this question with something I learned from my son, John, who is now building a successful career in sales. At some point in his sales training, he was taught the acronym, FORM. This is a method by which the salespersons (or fundraisers!) show a genuine interest in their prospects first before they move on to anything about their products or services. So the salesperson first asks about the prospect's **Family**; then he or she talks about the prospects **Occupation**; and then he or she asks questions about the prospect's **Recreation** or other pastimes. Only after he or she is comfortable that genuine concern has been demonstrated for the prospect as a real person with hopes and aspirations does the successful sales professional begin to speak about the **Message** of the sale or service.

This formula, or something like it, can help the new major gift fundraisers to gain the fluency they need to become effective in their interventions with donor prospects. Obviously, such fluency comes easier to some than to others. But it is a skill that can definitely be learned. What cannot be learned, however, is an essential genuine, sincere interest in people – all people. This interest we already have, or we would not be working or volunteering for a non-profit charitable organization in the first place.

Step Five: Invest: Now comes the hard part – at least for most of us. It is the time in the major gift process to actually ask for a large gift. We have identified legitimate prospects; we assessed their interest in our cause and now know why they give; the prospects now feel that our organization is theirs because they are truly involved in it; and we have intervened in their lives enough to know their real interests and what may motivate them to give a more substantial gift than they have ever given before. How do we go about making the ask?

First of all, I am pleased to report from my own experience that you may not have to actually ask for a major gift. It may just happen somewhere in the first four steps. This happened many times in my career. Let me cite two examples. First, there was a gentleman living in Wyoming, a few hundred miles from the Chapter Office. He was in the habit of making $250 to $500 annual gifts. I always called to thank him for these gifts, and we became pretty well acquainted over the telephone. I learned about him, his family, his arthritis, and about his very quiet life. We were probably at the "Intervention" step, and, frankly, I had made a preliminary conclusion that a request for a much larger gift was probably not appropriate. But one time he called me to say he had decided to cash in some bonds to allow him to make a large gift to the Arthritis Foundation. A few days later a check arrived from him in the amount of almost $40,000, a truly exceptional gift for him!

The second example resulted in a much larger amount of money. This was about a wonderful couple that was making regular annual gifts of $5,000 to $10,000. I had gotten to know them both very well, and she was now an active volunteer in our work. I knew of their strong interest in arthritis research and was planning to invite them to meet with the head of the rheumatology research laboratory at the local university. Then I received a telephone invitation to join them for lunch at their country club. It was an enjoyable lunch, full of friendly conversation. But, before it concluded, he handed me a few stock certificates, with ownership transferred over to the Arthritis Foundation. When I asked how much the certificates might be worth, he responded about $225,000. When I went on to ask for what they would like their gift to be spent, they responded that they hoped we could spend it on arthritis research. They had definitely beat me to the punch! But at least I was right about the direction I was going in the major gift process.

I guarantee that, if the non-profit charitable organization genuinely engages its major donor prospects in the Six I,s, it will have experiences like the two above without actually having to ask for major gifts. Moreover, I am also sure that, as these prospects are involved in this process, their annual gifts will increase, for example, from $250 to $500, from $500 to $1,000, from $1,000 to $2,000, and so on when they are asked to renew their annual support. People appreciate the fact that the non-profit organization is taking an interest in them and will respond in these positive ways – and without being specifically asked to do so.

We do, however, often have to make an actual request for a major gift. What is the best way to go about this? There are many effective ways I'm sure, but the way that I have found to be the most effective is to involve two people in the ask, one being a staff person, ideally the coordinator of the process for the specific prospect, and the other being a volunteer leader of the organization, ideally one who is known very well by the prospect. This asking team needs to spend some time in planning its approach and agreeing on the role that each will play. It usually is better for the actual asker to be the volunteer leader, especially because he or she usually has more leverage in the situation. But I have found that many volunteer leaders are not comfortable in this role, and, therefore, the staff person has to do this important task. In any event, there has to be firm agreement on the amount to be asked for and the purpose for which the major gift is sought.

Actually asking for a large amount of money is never easy, either for a volunteer leader or for a staff person. This is true even after thorough preparation by the asking team and even after a well-orchestrated and long process. What often saves the situation and serves to make the ask easier is the expressed awareness of the prospect. By this I mean that the conversation often goes like this: After the usual small talk that happens among friends over lunch or whatever the situation might be, it is often the prospect that actually gets to the point by saying something like, "I know that you are here for a reason." This will cause the asking team to get right to the point as well and to make the actual request. And, hopefully, largely because of the professional work that has gone on before this critical moment, the response will be in the affirmative.

But what does the asking team do if the response to its request is an unexpected "No?" Is this not the reason why we find such situations to be so difficult in the first place? We are afraid of receiving negative answers. And we are afraid because we don't know what to say when we receive one. I must admit that I struggled mightily with this issue until I read Jerold Panas' book, cited previously in this chapter, Finders Keepers. Chapter 5 of that wonderful little book is entitled "The Four Magic Questions." (3) Jerold here proposes what the asking team or individual fundraiser can do when the dreaded "No" is received. In so doing, he makes the point that the "No" really means "Later" or at least "Maybe."

Let me summarize the advice that Jerold Panas offers. When the "No" is heard, the asking team needs to immediately follow up with the first magic question: **"Is it the organization?"** In other words, is the reason why the prospect gave a negative answer the organization itself and its mission? Is there truly a lack of interest on the part of the prospect – or at least not enough interest – to cause the person to dig deeply into his or her resources to make the major gift that has been requested? If the prospect responds "Yes" to this question, then there is really nowhere else to go. We have requested a major gift from the wrong person, or we have done a terrible job of creating enough interest in the prospect for our cause. Granted, the latter case may lead to a "Maybe," but for now we have simply failed. Thankfully, receiving a "Yes" to this magic question is rarely the case. Usually the person will say something like this: "Oh, no. You have a wonderful organization, and I would love to support it."

Now comes the second magic question: **"Is it the program?"** In other words, is the reason why the prospect answered "No" to the request simply the fact that we asked him or her to support a specific aspect or project of our mission in which the prospect is not very interested? If the response is "Yes" to this question, we clearly have missed the mark, but, thankfully, we have somewhere else to go. Perhaps we have asked the person to help finance program A, but he or she is really interested in program B. Or perhaps we have asked for a large gift to support a capital project, but the prospect really is more interested in an on-going program. However, the prospect is more likely to answer "No," and he or she may go on to say that there is strong interest in the specific program or project.

Then we ask the third magic question: **"Is it the amount?"** In other words, have we asked for too much (or too little!)? Almost never will a prospect respond that we have asked for too little. We probably often do, but the prospect is not very likely to tell us so. More often the prospect may tell us that he or she would love to give what we have asked, but is not able to do so. Thus, if the answer is "Yes" that we have asked for too much, we have somewhere to go. We can then ask – and comfortably so – what amount would be more in line with what the prospect has in mind. And just as often the prospect will respond "No" that we have not asked for too much. The prospect may even go on to say that such an amount has been given by him or her to other organizations in the past. This response also gives us somewhere to go in the conversation.

We go on to the last magic question (At this point in my graduate school lecture, one of my students invariably interjects that the last question can only be: "Is it me?"), which is: **"Is it the timing?"** If the conversation has gone along this far, an affirmative response about the particular timing is almost the only one possible. Some circumstance in the prospect's life is making the major contribution an impossibility at this moment. Perhaps large tuition payments for children or grandchildren are due now. Or perhaps some investments have gone sour for a while. Whatever the reason may be – and the prospect may or may not share the specific reason – the asking team has an obvious direction to go in the discussion. We can comfortably ask when a better time might be. And, without a doubt, the prospect will respond clearly to such a question.

In my opinion, knowing about these four magic questions overcomes the last legitimate obstacle to being willing to ask someone for a large major gift. We really have no good reason to be nervous or reluctant about it. I remember once in my career, when I was feeling nervous about asking someone for a contribution, I expressed my anxiety to a Board member, who happened to be an excellent fundraiser. His response was immediate: "Why are you nervous? You're not asking for money for yourself!" It is very hard to argue against such logic. If we are truly committed to our cause, if we really know what a difference a prospect's contribution will make in people's lives, then we should not be nervous or reluctant to move forward. If we still are, I submit that we should not be involved in the major gift process in the first place.

Step Six: Influence: The final step in the major gift process, which has as its purpose the beginning of the process again with another prospect, should flow very naturally. Once the non-profit charitable organization has taken a person through the first five steps, and a positive result has taken place, the new major donor is now a real friend of the organization. We need to capitalize on this friendship by asking him or her if there is someone – or more than one – who might be recommended to join him or her as a major donor. If appropriate, we can ask him or her to introduce us to the potential donor or donors. Such an introduction is a most effective first step in beginning a new relationship.

Major Donor Recognition

Before closing this chapter on major gifts, it is important to talk about a most important aspect of any major gift program – donor recognition. Every contributor to a non-profit charitable organization, in any amount, deserves to receive an appropriate, personal expression of gratitude from that organization. And, the sooner this expression of thanks is made, the better it is and the more it is appreciated by the donor. This is especially true when it comes to major donors.

I suggest that every major donor should receive a telephone call from an important leader of the organization, ideally the Chair of the Board or Staff Executive, as soon as possible after the gift is made or received. We should strive to make this call of gratitude within 24 hours of the gift. This should be followed within a few days by a personal letter of thanks, containing an official receipt from the organization. There should be nothing "canned" about this letter. The major donor needs to feel that every word in the letter has been written just for him or her.

Another almost universal way to acknowledge the gift of a major donor is to list him or her among other donors in the annual report or other public documents of the organization according to levels of support. For example, those giving over $100,000 should be listed first. These are followed by those giving over $50,000. Then come those giving over $25,000, and so on. Very few major donors object to such listings. But, if some do say that they prefer not to be listed in any public documents, their wishes must be respected, of course.

We need to do much more than these rather standard ways to acknowledge support from exceptionally generous donors to our charitable organizations, but the additional steps we take must be truly individualized. I believe that all major donors enjoy being recognized – even if they state that they do not wish any recognition – provided that it is done appropriately and in ways that are meaningful to them. That is why, for example, you may wish to consult with the children or close friends of the donors about this issue before moving forward. And you never want the major donors themselves to be surprised by what you do. When asked directly about a particular form of recognition, even if they initially say something like "You really don't have to do anything," you can usually tell if what you plan will be enjoyed or not.

There are many different and effective ways to recognize the extreme thoughtfulness of major donors. These include naming buildings or parts of buildings after them, listing them with others like them on plaques on walls, and other similar standard practices. But I contend that a high level of creativity is in order here. For example, we might institute a new annual service award to be named after the donor and make him or her the first recipient of it. Or we might write and publish an article about the donor's exceptional contribution and what that contribution will accomplish in a publication of a professional group in which the donor is a member. A small intimate dinner among close friends, relatives, and family members of the donor is also a good idea. We shouldn't put limits around our creativity. I was challenged once at a seminar by a speaker on this topic who claimed that every major donor should be thanked and recognized at least seven times in seven different ways! That's quite a challenge, isn't it? And it is a great idea.

Bullet Summary

◆ Major gift fundraising should flow naturally from the annual giving and special event programs conducted by non-profit charitable organizations and be an essential part of their total fundraising effort, even if it is done in only a limited way.

◆ A major giving program is a definitive process, conducted with present or prospective donors to the organization, which seeks exceptionally generous gifts from individuals and usually takes from six months to two years to materialize.

◆ A designated staff person or volunteer leader must specifically coordinate the major giving process for each donor prospect, although the active assistance of other representatives of the non-profit charitable organization is often employed.

◆ The first step of six steps in the major giving process is to **identify** a person who has the capability and interest in the organization's mission to make such a contribution.

◆ The second step in the process is to discover the specific **interest** of the prospect in our mission and to learn what may motivate that person to make an exceptional gift.

◆ The third step is to actually **involve** the prospect in the work of the organization, so much so that the person now feels that he or she is a vital part of the organization.

◆ The fourth step is to meaningfully **intervene** in the lives of the donor prospects to demonstrate that the organization is as much interested in them as they are now interested in the non-profit charitable organization.

◆ The fifth step is to effectively ask the prospect to **invest** in the mission of the organization in an exceptionally generous way. An asking team, composed of a volunteer leader friend of the prospect and a high-level staff person, can best undertake this task.

◆ The sixth and final step is to request that the new major donor use his or her **influence** to lead the non-profit charitable organization to other prospects that may wish to make major gifts.

♦ Major donors need to be appropriately thanked and individually recognized for their generosity.

Conclusion

Chapter 10 has discussed the ways in which every non-profit charitable organization can implement a major giving program – a program that for a long time was almost exclusively used by hospitals, universities, and other large institutions. If we do not put such a program into operation, even to a limited degree, we are missing a tremendous opportunity to find support for our missions in large amounts and at very low cost. Now we move on to the subject of planned giving, a fundraising program that enables donors to non-profit organizations to provide support for our missions long after their deaths.

(1) Jerold Panas, Finders Keepers, 1999, Bonus Books, Chicago, p. 4.

(2) Nicole Lewis, "Wealthy People Say Tax Breaks Don't Affect Their Giving," The Chronicle of Philanthropy, Internet Report, 10/06.

(3) Jerold Panas, Op. Cit., Pp. 102-111.

Suggested Reading

Burk, op.cit., pp. 115-136.

Ciconte and Jacob, op.cit., pp. 121-156.

Panas, Finders Keepers: Lessons I've Learned about Dynamic Fundraising, Bonus Books, Chicago, 1999.

Panas, Mega Gifts: Who Gives Them and Who Gets Them, Emerson and Church Publishers, Medfield, MA, 2006.

Sturtevant, The Artful Journey, Bonus Books, Chicago, 1997.

Chapter 11: Call My Attorney and Trust Officer:

Bequests and Planned Giving in Non-Profit Organizations

Several years ago, I visited a long-time donor in her small, modest condo in downtown Denver. She was well into her 80's and severely disabled by arthritis. Her annual gifts over many years remained at $25, but she never missed in sending her contribution promptly when she received her renewal notice. She told me that she owned some stock and that the Arthritis Foundation would receive part of the stock value upon her death from a trust she had established. Then she insisted that I call her attorney and trust officer when I returned to my office. She wanted them to know me so that the distribution from the trust would come to the Arthritis foundation as soon as possible after her death. I was uncomfortable in following her wishes, but did so. She died a year or two later, and we immediately received a copy of her trust document. I was surprised to learn then that we would receive, along with equal amounts to two other charitable organizations, about $150,000!

This story about a thoughtful lady, who didn't want others to suffer with arthritis as she had, illustrates for me what I have always thought about bequests and planned giving. It represents the **ultimate in generosity**. For someone to work hard for all his or her life and accumulate some treasure, no matter how big or small, and then upon death to share that treasure – or a significant portion of it – with a charitable organization to carry on its mission is an exceedingly generous act.

As mentioned earlier in this text, bequests and planned giving make up about 8% of total philanthropic giving in the United States, as reported by the Giving USA Foundation. That percentage is even higher when we look at the total fundraising results in health related organizations. For example, throughout my career with the Arthritis Foundation, bequests and planned giving consistently represented about a third of our public support both at local and national levels of the Foundation. I am convinced that any non-profit charitable organization can receive significant contributions in this way.

Those organizations that are successful in receiving substantial dollars from bequests and planned giving see this method of fundraising as a natural outgrowth of strong annual giving and major giving programs. For example, they see a person who regularly makes a $1,000 annual gift to be capable of major gifts a few times in his or her life of perhaps $100,000. And in their view this same person, if cultivated and stewarded appropriately over several years, may choose to include the same charitable organization in his or her estate plan for $1,000,000. These numbers, of course, are very general in nature. But they do illustrate the real potential of a lifetime donor to a charitable cause.

The purpose of this chapter is to convince the reader that this method of fundraising is well within the reach of any non-profit charitable organization. To accomplish this task, the chapter will proceed in the following way. First, I will discuss the various kinds of planned giving instruments a donor may choose. Then, I will talk about the relationship between tax deductions and this fundraising method. Third, I will review the characteristics of the most likely prospects for planned giving. Fourth, I will take a look at the false obstacles that stand in the way of the implementation of this method of fundraising in many organizations. Fifth, I will outline some simple and inexpensive methods of promoting planned giving among our donors. Finally, I will present a relatively new aspect of a planned giving program, namely the recognition of donors while they are still alive.

Methods of Planned Giving

There is no doubt that the field of estate planning – or the task of planning the distribution of a person's assets upon his or her death – is a very complex and challenging endeavor. In fact, many highly educated and skilled professionals, such as attorneys, trust officers, and financial planners, work exclusively in this field. But this does not mean that a non-profit charitable organization needs to have this professional expertise to successfully operate a planned giving fundraising program. Our primary responsibility is to motivate our donors to consider including our organizations in their estate plans, not to help them to design and implement their specific plans. There is a huge arsenal of estate planning instruments available to people today, and there is no need for us to be knowledgeable about them all. When our donors ask about them, we should simply refer them to their financial consultants to give them the technical information and advice they need.

Among the many estate planning instruments available to our donors are bequests, trusts, annuities, individual retirement accounts, and insurance policies. All have particular advantages for specific situations. But, in my experience, well over 80% of the planned giving income we received came in the form of a simple bequest. Most of the rest came in the form of a trust or an annuity. If we have a basic understanding of these primary methods, we can talk with enough intelligence with our donors about the vast majority of the alternatives they are considering.

A **bequest** results from a person's Last Will and Testament, in which a person predetermines how his or her assets are to be distributed following death. Through a Will, a person can decide to bequeath some assets to a charity in one of two ways. The first is through a specific bequest, in which the Will simply states that a certain amount of money or other asset is to be given to a charitable organization upon death. The second way is called a residuary bequest, in which the person states in the Will that specific amounts of money or other assets are to be given to family members and others and then, from whatever is left or the 'residuary," a certain charitable organization (or organizations) is to receive a percentage. I found the residuary bequest to be very common.

In any event, because the Will becomes a public document when it is admitted to probate following death, the charitable organization mentioned in the Will should receive a copy of it from the attorney administering the estate. The attorney has to officially notify all persons and organizations mentioned in the Will that they have an interest in it, and a copy of the Will should be attached to that notice. (If it was not, I would always immediately request it.) Then the charitable group can determine the amount of the bequest, if it is specific, or at least the percentage, if it is residuary. In either case, after some time, the attorney will inform interested parties of the total assets in the estate through the publication of an inventory, and from that inventory the residuary beneficiaries can make some estimate of their interest. The process of probate on average takes about a year, and, when the process is completed, the charitable organization can expect to receive its bequest.

A **trust** can take many forms, and all are quite technical in nature. For this reason, if ever a donor expresses an interest in establishing a trust, I recommend strongly that he or she be referred directly to an attorney who is an expert in this field. Due to its complexity, a trust usually costs much more time and money to establish than a Will, but the principal reason why a person might choose to establish one is that his or her estate settlement after death can avoid probate and, theoretically at least, be settled much quicker with much less public scrutiny. My experience testifies that charitable organizations are receiving more and more contributions through trusts, but that bequests are still the most dominant way by far.

The last method of planned giving I want to highlight here is the **charitable gift annuity**. This not only results in a significant contribution to the charitable organization upon the donor's death, but it can also be very beneficial to the donor himself or herself while still living. The ideal prospect for the charitable gift annuity is the donor who is wealthy in assets and yet still is concerned about having enough income to live on for the rest of his or her life. If such a donor contributes an asset to a charitable organization in the form of a charitable gift annuity, depending on the value of the asset and the age of the donor, the organization will guarantee a certain level of income to the donor for the rest of his or her life. And usually there are tax advantages to the donor at the time of the contribution. But the organization cannot take full possession of the asset's value until the donor actually dies.

Let me cite an example to clarify these features of the charitable gift annuity. An elderly widow has a modest but sufficient income from Social Security and a retirement program, but is living in a totally owned home once purchased for $50,000 with a current market value of $350,000 – a relatively common circumstance in these days. She concludes that the home is now too much for her, she wants to sell it, and she has found a modest apartment to which she would like to move. With the added burden of rental payments, she fears that she will no longer have enough income. Clearly she has many financial options at this point to create the income she needs. But one would be a charitable gift annuity. If she would give her home to a charitable organization she cares about, she would enjoy an immediate tax deduction relative to the market value of her home, and the organization would guarantee her an 8% return on her home value or $28,000 per year for as long as she lives. Now she is comfortable that she has the regular income she needs, has created some additional income through a tax deduction, and now has the satisfaction that she is doing something meaningful for others through her gift to charity. The charitable organization most probably would then sell the home and invest the money in something secure and with the potential to generate the income of 8% per year required to remit regular payments back to the donor. Finally, whatever is left of the original $350,000, will revert to the charitable organization for its use upon her death.

Armed with this general knowledge about various planned giving instruments, the non-profit charitable organization can now proceed to speak intelligently to its donors about opportunities presented and refer interested donors to their attorneys for the legal and complex details that may be required.

Tax Deductions and Planned Giving

Currently there is quite a debate going on among politicians, philanthropic leaders, and tax experts in this country about the effect of estate taxes on charitable contributions through bequests and other methods of planned giving. Some argue that a reduction in estate taxes, or an elimination thereof, would have little or no effect on and may even increase the amount of charitable giving upon death. Others argue the opposite point of view and assert that estate taxes encourage charitable giving at death and their reduction or elimination would have a severely deleterious effect on such giving. The Chronicle of Philanthropy published a good summary of such arguments a short time ago, with the latter argument offered first:

> Jon M. Bakija and William G. Gale of the Urban-Brookings Tax Policy Center in Washington …have estimated that repealing the estate tax would reduce charitable giving by at least $10-billion annually. They say wealthy people would no longer be motivated to make tax-free charitable gifts as a way to reduce the portion of their estate subject to federal taxes.

> But other scholars such as Paul G. Schervish and John J. Havens of the Boston College Center on Wealth and Philanthropy have argued that repealing the estate tax could increase charitable giving. Many wealthy people, they note, intentionally limit the amount they leave to heirs; an estate-tax repeal would leave them with more disposable income and other assets to transfer to charities. (1)

I believe that the truth in this matter can be found in the middle of these two arguments. Like was stated in a similar discussion in the previous chapter on major gifts, I am convinced that the tax deductibility of charitable giving is not the primary motivator to the donor. The primary motivator is a desire to help others through the support of a charitable cause. But, once that motivation is present, I have found that tax deductibility often encourages donors to increase their contributions. This is true in major giving and planned giving both. With this in mind, as a non-profit charitable organization tries to promote its planned giving program among its supporters, it should first appeal to the donors' charitable instincts and only secondarily to any tax benefit that may be involved.

Planned Giving Prospects

Who among our donors should we focus on as potential planned giving contributors? Some obvious examples come to mind with the realization first that they must be people with a demonstrated interest in our cause. They are the past and present members of our Board of Directors, active volunteer corps, and staff. Added to this group are all regular donors at all levels. As a further qualification, I would suggest that they are supporters and donors with no children or who have children that are doing well themselves. And, to qualify them even further, I would focus on the group that has provided steady support for a very long time, and I emphasize again that this does not have to be a high dollar amount of support. I believe strongly that "steady support for a very long time" is the most critical factor of all. A final qualification to be added is that women in the above categories should be subjects of our focus, only because they increasingly tend to outlive their spouses.

I would like to give two examples from my career that illustrate the above qualifications. One woman was a faithful $10 donor for many years. Much to our surprise, when she died we received notice that she had bequeathed her home to us, which we were able to sell for about $40,000! Another woman was also a loyal donor of many years, with gifts ranging from $20 to $100. Upon her death, we received a copy of a very complex trust instrument in which she stated that she was sharing her estate with three charitable organizations including the Arthritis Foundation. Again, much to our surprise, a few months later we learned that the three organizations were to receive $1.5 million each from her trust! This was the largest planned gift we received during my 25-year career. And it is important to note that in both instances the donors were primarily motivated by the fact that they did not want others to suffer with arthritis as they had during their lives. Yes, indeed, a planned gift is the ultimate in generosity.

False Obstacles to a Planned Giving Program

I have found that far too many non-profit charitable organizations do not have a planned giving fundraising program because they see several obstacles to its implementation, which, at least in my opinion, are quite false. These obstacles usually center around three factors. Let's take a look at each one.

The **first** is about the **staffing** of the program. Many organizations feel uncomfortable in launching a planned giving program because they feel that they do not have qualified staff to run it and cannot afford to hire such staff. My initial response to this false obstacle is that I have seen several non-profit organizations, including our organization early in my executive career, receive substantial dollars through planned giving without having any specifically qualified staff at all. And they did so by simply implementing the simple and inexpensive methods that I will describe in the next section of this chapter. There is no doubt that the presence of specifically qualified staff will definitely enhance the planned giving program, as I learned later on in my career when we had the benefit of a regional staff expert, but such a staff person is not essential to the initial success of the program.

The **second** false obstacle is the perceived **technical knowledge** that is necessary to start a planned giving program. I addressed this obstacle earlier in this chapter and will only repeat here that our basic responsibilities are to motivate our supporters to consider such gifts, to have a rudimentary knowledge of the most popular planned giving instruments, namely, bequests, trusts, and annuities, and to refer our interested donors on to attorneys and other experts to deal with the complex details of these instruments.

The **third** false obstacle – and perhaps the most significant one – is the fact that planned giving **income is not immediate**. Many non-profit charitable organizations find themselves so concerned about creating immediate income to keep their doors open and service programs going that they ignore making any effort to secure planned giving income. This is a huge mistake. First of all, income from bequests and other planned giving instruments tends to "mature" (This is the jargon in the industry!) within 5 to 7 years after the donors make their decisions about them. In other words, the average planned giving donor usually waits to late in life to make such decisions and actually dies within 5 to 7 years after those decisions. That is really not a very long time. Another important implication of allowing this false obstacle to rule the organization's fundraising behavior is that the organization may never get out of its exclusive focus on the here and now in its fundraising efforts. As a result, the organization may never be able to create the necessary financial reserve position that can create the stability it needs to truly carry out its mission. In my actual experience, it was planned giving income – and only such income – that created and maintained a strong reserve position for our Chapter.

Simple and Inexpensive Methods

Starting a planned giving program in a non-profit charitable organization is really quite simple and inexpensive. Six methods come to mind. They all are like "drilling for oil," in that you'll never know when one will stir an interest in a donor or volunteer.

The **first** thing to do is simply to **let our donors and volunteers know that we are interested in receiving income in this way**. This can be accomplished, to cite an example, by including a statement like "Remember the _____ (your charitable organization) in your Will" at the bottom of your stationery. We took this a step further and included such a statement on every piece of literature we published and/or distributed. It's been amazing to me to see how such a simple thing can begin the thought processes in our supporters that eventually lead them to taking some planned giving action.

The **second** method is to write and/or publish motivating **articles on planned giving** in our printed or e-mail newsletters to our donors and volunteers. In these articles we can talk about bequests and planned giving as being the "ultimate in generosity," as ways to carry a "lasting legacy of support" for the organization's mission, and so on.

A **third** method is to **give recognition to planned giving donors** in our newsletters. This can be done in two ways. One is to insert boxes within the text of the newsletter containing statements of gratitude, such as: "We are grateful to _____ (name of deceased donor) for contributing $_____ towards our mission in his or her Will." Or we can write short articles about planned giving donors, about their financial contributions, and what we can accomplish or have accomplished because of their generosity. Over the years I became convinced that such publication was very motivating to readers to start thinking what they might be able to do in this regard.

A **fourth** method follows from the two above, and it is the **insertion of a coupon** following an article on planned giving through which a reader can indicate an interest in this means of giving. By completing and returning the coupon, the interested person can indicate an interest in planned giving or request a brochure on the subject.

This leads to a **fifth** method, which is the **purchase and distribution of brochures on various planned giving subjects.** Such brochures, written on bequests, trusts, annuities, and other planned giving subjects are readily and inexpensively purchased from several publishers. These brochures can even be individualized to any non-profit charitable organization by having the name and contact information of the organization inserted on the front or back. Once obtained, these brochures can then be advertised as being available to interested people or distributed widely among our donors and volunteers in any ways that we choose.

The **sixth** and final method to be considered here is the **sponsorship of planned giving seminars** for our donors and volunteers. Again, this is not at all expensive to do, largely because the speakers, namely, attorneys and trust officers, are relatively easy to recruit and will not charge for their service. This is seen by them to be a legitimate way to advertise their professional services among interested people. These seminars are offered as a service by our organization to our donors. The speakers will primarily cover subjects like the importance of having a Will, how to preserve assets for children, the various methods of planned giving and the advantages of each, and the tax benefits resulting from including donations to charitable organizations in the estate plans. Hopefully, the speakers will use your organization as an example as they illustrate this latter point. We would hold such seminars about two or three times per year, perhaps attended by 10 or 15 people, and invariably we would learn of at least one planned gift to our organization resulting from each one.

I find it hard to see how the implementation of these six methods could cost more than $10,000 per year and demand as much as 10% of a professional staff person's time. In fact, for a few years of my career, we were blessed with the volunteer service of one of our Board members who was interested and became educated in planned giving and led our efforts in the six methods described above. During this time period, I personally, as the Staff Executive, was able to devote much less than 5% of my time to this program. And it was done very well, too!

Recognition of Planned Giving Donors While Alive

The final topic to be covered in this chapter is the recognition of planned giving donors while they are still alive and before their gifts actually materialize. Before we instituted such an activity, I was continually frustrated by our inability to express any gratitude at all for such gifts, even to the surviving families of planned giving donors. When we were notified by an attorney about the death of a donor and our inclusion in his or her Will or other instrument, I would immediately contact the attorney to see if there were family members with whom I could express some thanks. Most often, the attorney would respond that I should do nothing, largely because at least some family members resented the fact that some of the decedent's estate was now not available to them! And even in those few times in which I was able to contact the decedent's family, I was still dissatisfied that I was unable to express gratitude to the donor himself or herself.

To counteract this frustration, many non-profit charitable organizations have now established special societies or clubs for intended planned giving donors. In our case it was called the "Discovery Alliance" to indicate to the donor members that they were now part of an elite group that would eventually allow us to reach our final objective of finding the causes and cures of the many different forms of arthritis. Membership in this alliance was extended to any persons who indicated to us that they had included our organization in their estate plans, regardless of the amount. (We would never ask for the amount.) Then these generous people were given a lapel pin and a framed award certificate. We would also invite them to our annual meetings as our guests and, if they chose to attend, give them special recognition while there. An added benefit to such a recognition program is the fact that it was motivating to others to be included in the same elite group.

Bullet Summary

♦ Bequests and Planned Giving represent the ultimate in generosity on the part of individual donors to non-profit charitable organizations.

♦ The implementation of a successful planned giving program is well within reach of almost any non-profit organization of any size and purpose.

♦ About 80% of planned gifts come in the form of bequests, with most of the others resulting from trusts or annuities – the basic understanding of which is easily understood.

♦ There are tax deductions resulting from including a charitable organization in one's estate plans, but these are not the primary motivators for most donors. Rather a commitment to the charitable organization's mission is usually the primary motivator.

♦ The most likely prospects for charitable planned giving are long-time, regular donors in any amounts, and among these the most likely are women because they tend to outlive their spouses.

♦ Many non-profit charitable organizations ignore the possibilities of implementing a planned giving program, largely because they allow false obstacles to get in their way.

♦ There are six simple and inexpensive methods involved with instituting a successful planned giving program, and these can be readily implemented by almost any non-profit charitable organization.

♦ In recent times, charitable organizations have found ways to recognize and thank planned giving donors while they are still alive. These ways are not only satisfying to the donors themselves, but also motivating to others to consider making planned gifts to charity.

Conclusion

This chapter concludes the sections of the book describing ways to raise funds from individuals to support the missions of non-profit charitable organizations. As we have seen, such fundraising represents 84% of the total amount of current philanthropy in the United States. The final two chapters will cover the remaining two sources of charitable giving, namely, corporations and foundations. Chapter 12 will talk about raising dollars from corporations, which are responsible for providing about 5% of the country's philanthropic dollars.

(1) Holly Hall, "Estate Taxes Effect of Giving May Not Matter So Much, New Analysis Finds," The Chronicle of Philanthropy, December 10, 2006, p. 33.

Suggested Reading

Ciconte and Jacob, op.cit., pp. 319-335.

Chapter 12: **What's In It For Us?**

Corporate Fundraising in Non-Profit Organizations

Oftentimes during my career, after I had made a proposal for funds to a corporate leader, it was not at all unusual for that leader to sit back in his or her chair and ask the question: "If we do give money to your organization, what's in it for us?" Thus, what I gave emphasis to in Chapter 7 – that fundraising is a voluntary **exchange** among people – is frequently quite openly stated by a corporate leader in this context. (By the way, I have never heard an individual donor express a desire for some exchange so literally, although the desire for something in return may be just as real for the individual as well.) But we should not be surprised by such candor. A business must justify a contribution to a charitable organization by expecting something in return that may benefit the ultimate goal of the enterprise, namely the enhancement of profit for owners and stockholders.

I have seen graduate students, charitable organization leaders, and especially business representatives become quite disappointed when they learn that corporate gifts make up only about 5% of the total philanthropy in the United States. My immediate response is to remind them that 5% of $306 billion is still a lot of money! I then go on to say that it is perhaps surprising that corporations give any money at all to charitable causes. One could easily make the case that corporations could be very comfortable in staying true to their primary purpose in producing profit for their owners, while at the same time seeing contributions as being extraneous to this primary purpose. Nonetheless – and thankfully I might add – many corporate leaders do not see charitable contributions as extraneous to their primary purpose. That is the reason that I begin this chapter with a discussion about why some corporations choose to support charitable groups.

With these thoughts in mind, the order of the chapter will be as follows. First, as just stated, I will discuss the reasons why some corporations contribute to non-profit charitable organizations. Then, I will emphasize the point that corporations have several "pots of money" from which support can be sought. Third, I will consider a relatively recent development in corporate fundraising, namely, cause related marketing. Fourth, I will discuss some possible negative aspects of raising money from businesses. Finally, I will close with some comments about the important strategy of having corporate representatives on the Boards of Directors of non-profit organizations.

Why Corporations Support Charitable Organizations

Several reasons come to mind that provide justification for a for-profit business to support a non-profit charitable organization. And it is important to note that all of them relate in one way or another and more or less to the enhancement of profit. The first and very obvious reason is to increase sales. The example I often use with my students to illustrate this is about two plasma television sets of comparable value offered by two companies for the same price of $2,000. But one company advertises that it will make a contribution to a charitable organization for every set sold, while the other company makes no such offer. When I ask the students which plasma TV they would purchase, they respond enthusiastically that they would choose the first one, especially if the charitable cause was a positive one in their minds. The other reasons are not so clearly seen as relating to the profit motive, but the relationship is there nonetheless.

A corporation may give contributions to charity simply because it wants to have a positive community image among its potential customers. It may also see such support as creating a positive business environment, especially when the contributions are given to organizations that enhance the overall well being of a community. Contributing to cultural charitable groups may increase the company's competitiveness in attracting qualified personnel to move their families to the area. And the support of educational programs may help to create an appropriate work force for the corporation in its community.

Some corporations allow their executives to distribute a certain amount of charitable dollars in accordance with their own personal interests. Such a practice may give a highly respected executive additional job satisfaction and assist the corporation in retaining its executive leadership. Special events of charitable organizations provide many opportunities for corporations to increase their visibility through various levels of sponsorship. And with all corporate solicitations, fundraising groups need to recognize that their success will increase the more they can demonstrate that they will raise the visibility of the corporation among its own real and potential customers and in the area in which these customers live. Without such a demonstration, the success of any solicitation is very slim, indeed.

Two recent studies have substantiated that charitably minded companies actually do increase their bottom lines. The first, published in 2006 by researchers at the New York University Stern School of Business and the University of Texas at Dallas School of Management, concluded that "corporate charitable contributions are effective in enhancing revenues in the 'consumer sectors,' such as retailers and financial services." The other, published in 2007 by Dover Management, "a company that operates a mutual fund that invests in corporations committed to charitable giving," found that "companies with a solid link between giving and operating earnings outperformed the Standard & Poor's 500 Index by 3.5 percentage points over five years." (1) Knowing about these study findings may be very useful to us in our charitable solicitations of businesses.

Corporate "Pots of Money"

The fundraising efforts of non-profit charitable organizations can be directed at several different "pots of money" within many corporations. First of all, some larger corporations have established actual charitable foundations separate from themselves to handle their contributions. (These will be discussed further in the next chapter.) Others have established employee committees through which they support charitable groups. These committees are given budgets to use in making their funding decisions. Non-profit organizations need to make formal application to these committees. It seems to me that this is a wise way for corporations to carry out their charitable giving. Not only do they achieve the objectives among their real and potential customers that were described above, they also improve employee morale through the operation of such committees. And oftentimes these charitable committee budgets are increased by employee contributions that are then matched by the corporation. So the whole process becomes a win-win situation for everyone involved, including the charitable organizations in the community that apply and receive needed funding.

An increasing number of corporations in these days are carrying out something similar with their employees through matching gift programs. These corporations actually encourage and support employee charitable giving by matching the individual donations of their employees to the same organizations to which the employees have directed their gifts. Thus, the employees can complete company forms when they make their individual donations and send them along to the recipient organizations. The organizations, in turn, complete their half of the company forms verifying the employee donations and return them to the corporations. Then the corporations directly respond to the organizations with contributions of at least equal value. The interesting fact about such corporate matching programs is that many employees are unaware that they can increase the impact of their own charitable giving in this way. Therefore, it is important for charitable organizations to know which corporations in their respective service areas have such programs and then publish such information among their own donors. Otherwise the organizations may just be losing funds that they can easily acquire.

As mentioned above, charitable organizations may appeal directly to corporate executives who may have access to funds allocated by their employers to discretionary charitable budgets of the executives themselves. This is one instance in which having a corporate executive on the non-profit organization's Board is especially helpful. Oftentimes, only a corporate executive is aware of such discretionary budgets among his or her peers in other companies in the community.

Within many communities throughout the United States, corporations actually challenge and encourage other corporations to contribute to non-profit organizations. For example, for many years in Denver metropolitan area, there has been a "Two Percent Club." Membership in this club is restricted to those corporations that pledge to donate at least two percent of their net-profits to charity each year. Such practices tend to enhance the image of the business community as a whole in the local area, increase community spirit among those companies who participate, and help to create the positive business environment desired by all corporations. Non-profit organizations need to be aware of the corporations in their communities that are charitably minded in this way and find ways to be included in the distribution of such funds.

Generally speaking, however, marketing budgets of corporations are much larger than their charitable budgets. Non-profit charitable organizations that are astute in convincing corporations to use their marketing budgets to support them will tend to acquire a much larger portion of corporate dollars. Access to marketing budgets is reserved to those organizations that can demonstrate a connection to the same people that may be real or prospective customers of the corporations. I witnessed a relatively frequent example of this throughout my executive career. From time to time, various pharmaceutical companies would be about to launch new medications helpful to people with arthritis. At such times, we knew that the companies would be more open than usual to proposals to sponsor our programs. Our own policies would not allow us to directly or indirectly endorse such new medications, but we could advertise that a certain educational or service program was sponsored by _____ Pharmaceutical Company. In this way, while remaining true to our own policies and ethics, we were providing a real benefit to the companies involved by allowing their names to be associated with our work and among people with arthritis at critical marketing times.

Cause Related Marketing

This leads to a discussion about cause related marketing – a relatively new strategy utilized frequently in these days by corporations, but not without controversy in the philanthropic world. It seems to be generally agreed that cause related marketing began with the American Express Company several years ago. This company chose to be supportive of the renovation of the Statue of Liberty and used this as a marketing device. It advertised widely that it would make a financial contribution to the statue's renovation for every application received for a new American Express card. This proved to be a highly successful marketing strategy in that it apparently encouraged many more people than usual to make application.

Since this successful venture by the American Express Company, many other corporations have instituted such programs with many different charitable organizations and causes. For example, in 2005, when Hurricanes Katrina and Rita devastated large areas in the Southeastern United States, several corporations conducted promotions in which they pledged to make donations to various charitable organizations providing help to the victims of the hurricanes in recognition of the sale of their products or services. This has resulted in some controversy over the issue that some of the corporations failed to disclose in their advertising the exact amount that would be donated to charity upon a sale. As a result, government regulators in Louisiana and Mississippi have accused them of fraud when evidence of the specific amounts donated to the charitable cause was not produced. Such controversy not only tarnishes the image of the corporations involved, but also can do a lot of damage to the non-profit charitable organizations that are the recipients of the contributions, especially if people begin to feel that they are being "duped" to buy products or services on the promise that a significant portion of their purchase price is going to support an activity they want to support. (2)

In addition to the charges of fraud that have surfaced recently in regard to cause related marketing, for some time philanthropy leaders have raised concerns that this fundraising strategy is not appropriate because it is not "true" charitable giving on the part of corporations. I am of the opinion that such objections are a real stretch. As stated previously in this text, fundraising is a "voluntary exchange" in which both the donor and the recipient charity receive something. In the instance of cause related marketing, the money given is still voluntary on the part of the corporations, because they do not have to enter into an agreement with a charitable organization and promote their products and services in this manner. Also voluntary is the money used in the purchase by the buyer, provided the amount of the donation to charity is made explicit in the advertising. One could argue, I suppose, that the "exchange" to the corporation is made much too blatant in such transactions in that the profit motive is paramount. But I have little or no problem with this. Profit is the primary reason for a corporate enterprise. If profit can be pursued and income to a charitable organization results at the same time, then the transaction is good for everyone involved.

To conclude this discussion about cause related marketing, I encourage non-profit charitable organizations to be assertive in seeking out these kinds of opportunities to raise the dollars needed for their programs from corporations. As they do, however, I suggest that they make some critical judgments beforehand and insist on a few things in their negotiations with their prospective corporate partners:

1. Make sure that the prospective corporate partner is one in which there is a natural affinity to the charitable organization or at least one that sells products or services which are not contrary to the mission of the organization. The discussion about affinity in Chapter 9 in relation to corporate sponsorships of special events should be reviewed in this regard.

2. Ascertain that the corporate partner has a positive image among most people, realizing that the positive community image of the non-profit organization will now be at stake as well. No amount of success in fundraising, in my opinion, is worth the loss of a positive community image for the charitable organization.

3. Negotiate a specific and significant amount of contribution, at least on a percentage of sales basis, that will be given to the charitable organization. This amount must also be clearly and frequently stated in all advertising and promotional materials.

4. Insist upon the prerogative to review and approve all advertising and promotional materials that are produced for the marketing campaign, especially those items that contain mention of the charitable organization.

5. Seek to be protected from liability in the event of any suits or settlements that may result because of the improper implementation of the marketing campaign or the defects in the products or services provided by the corporation.

6. Have all contracts and agreements reviewed by the legal counsel of the charitable organization before they are signed.

If these and other precautionary measures are taken, cause related marketing and other similar partnerships with for-profit companies can be a regular, significant, and comfortable source of funds for many non-profit charitable organizations.

Possible Negative Aspects of Corporate Fundraising

The possible negative aspects involved with corporate fundraising usually flow from the fact that the one constant variable in the business world is **change**. Changes in personnel, in organizational structure, and in bottom-line business success or failure are commonplace. My experience tells me that this constant change, although it usually happens for the purpose of improving the companies involved and their profitability, most often does not benefit the charitable organizations that may be receiving regular support before the change. Let me illustrate this point with a few examples.

A charitable organization may have developed a strong relationship with a corporate CEO or other top-level manager and, because of this relationship, may receive regular contributions or other resources from that company. But what happens when the CEO or top-level manager moves on – an event that happens very frequently in the corporate world? Usually, in this instance, the charitable organization has to start all over with the new leadership personnel and may or may not ever reach the previous level of corporate support. The only way I know of to counteract this potential loss of revenue is to ask the departing CEO or top-level manager, before he or she actually leaves, to give emphasis to the importance of this charitable support with remaining management leaders and to ask that it be continued. Experience tells me, however, that the continuance of the same level of support is relatively unlikely, even when the departing organization contact person does try to help in this way. It would be a victory if even a diminished level of support is retained.

Another common change in the for-profit corporate world is merger. Such consolidation of resources and operations happens very frequently, and most often the primary focus is one of maximizing profit. During my career, our Chapter of the Arthritis Foundation was especially affected by mergers of banks, hospitals, and medical practice groups. For example, our annual golf tournament received sponsorship support from several individual banks, hospitals, and medical practice groups. When mergers happened among these entities – and they seemed to happen quite regularly – not only were we not able to successfully solicit the same level of sponsorship that we had received before from the now combined enterprises, but oftentimes we were unable to retain any level at all. This was especially true when the merger resulted in the corporate headquarters being in another city, and local corporate leaders were no longer empowered to make such sponsorship decisions.

A final illustration of the precariousness of corporate fundraising support is more general in nature. I have found that contributions from companies simply cannot be counted on from year to year. Whether this results from the rise and fall of business financial success, from the changing priorities and/or leadership in corporations, or from reactions to the course of events in life that engulf us all, the consequence is the same. Donor loyalty is just not found among corporations and their charitable contribution programs. For this reason, I again emphasize the point made many times throughout this text. Fundraising success year after year can only be built upon the regular contributions of individuals who have become a part of the constituency of our charitable organization. At best, corporate fundraisng can be an important source of significant, but irregular funds to support the missions of our organizations.

For-profit Corporate Leaders on Non-profit Boards

During my career, no one has taught me more about corporate fundraising than the for-profit business leaders who I have gotten to know largely through their service on the Board of Directors or on a fundraising committee of our charitable organization. They tend to know other corporate leaders and how other companies can best be approached for their support. Frankly, I have been amazed at how just one strategically placed telephone call from one business leader to another can easily result in a contribution or sponsorship. One might think that the high level of competition between businesses would prohibit such a spirit of cooperation. But I have found the opposite to be true. Evidently there is much respect among business competitors who are successful.

It is easy to see the inherent fundraising value of having for-profit leaders on non-profit Boards. The greater challenge lies in identifying corporate leaders who are willing to serve their communities in this way, recruiting them effectively, and keeping them involved. But an organization can overcome even this challenge. It seems to me that an ever-increasing number of corporate leaders look to service on non-profit Boards of Directors as something worthwhile for them personally and for their companies. In fact, many corporations actually encourage their executives to become involved in this way. Such involvement provides a community service dimension to their lives that they do not have in their business careers and tends to improve the images of their companies throughout the consumer community. Therefore, we have something to give to business leaders and their companies by inviting them to serve on our Boards. But keeping such leaders involved in our work may be the greater challenge. They tend to have very limited time to give, and what time they have they want to give in a business like way. So we should use their time strategically, that is, when their particular talents are actually needed. And, above all, we should never waste their time, by asking them to be involved in activities that are not specific to their interests and abilities. We will lose them if we do.

Bullet Summary

◆ Many for-profit corporations choose to support non-profit charitable organizations for several different reasons, but all of these reasons, either directly or indirectly, relate to their pursuit of profit.

◆ Corporations have several "pots of money" from which to solicit support for charitable causes. These sources of funds go beyond charitable contributions to include budgets for advertising and marketing.

◆ Cause related marketing, although controversial in nature, can be an acceptable way for charitable organizations to receive support from corporations, provided that it is done in thoughtful and ethical ways.

◆ Even though corporate fundraising can never become the dominant methodology in charitable development programs, it can still represent a significant, irregular source of funds.

◆ Having for-profit business leaders serve on the Boards and development committees of non-profit charitable organizations can enhance corporate fundraising programs.

Conclusion

Chapter 12 looked at corporate fundraising as a valuable adjunct to the central fundraising focus of non-profit charitable organizations, which clearly has to be on raising funds from individuals. Now it is time to complete the total picture of a comprehensive fundraising program by discussing the best ways to apply for and to receive grants from foundations – a stable and growing source of philanthropic dollars that represent 13% of the total charitable contributions in the United States.

(1) "Companies that give more to Charity are more Profitable, Study Finds," The Chronicle of Philanthropy, Internet Report, October 29, 2007.

(2) Peter Painpinto and Elizabeth Schwinn, "A Time to Thrive," The Chronicle of Philanthropy, April 5, 2007, pp. 21-22.

Suggested Reading

Ciconte and Jacob, op.cit., pp. 157-196.

Chapter 13: When You Know One Foundation:

Grant Writing in Non-Profit Organizations

In my course on fundraising at the University of Denver, when it's time to devote a class period to grant writing, I always invite program officers of foundations to speak and to respond to the questions of the graduate students. When the topic of the importance of doing research on foundations before submitting a grant application comes up, invariably one of the program officers states: "When you know one foundation, you know one foundation." In other words, the program officer is making the point that foundations are so different from each other – different in available funds, areas of interest, size of grants, grant cycles, methods of operation, application procedures, and people involved – that knowing something about one foundation helps very little, if at all, in learning about another foundation. Thus, doing extensive research on every foundation that may be appropriate for a particular grant application is not only an absolute necessity, but it also prevents a lot of frustration and extra work.

Charitable grant making by foundations, as indicated in the introductory section to this part of the book, currently represents about 13% of the total philanthropy in this country. And the total amount of foundation grant making appears to be growing significantly these days, largely due to the relatively new and exceptionally large amounts made available by very wealthy philanthropists, such as Bill and Melinda Gates, Warren Buffett, Ted Turner, and George Soros, all of whom choose to do most of their charitable giving through foundations. The total amount of foundation grants does not and most likely will never even approach the current 83% of total charitable giving provided by individuals, but, nonetheless, foundations will continue to be an important source of funds for the missions of non-profit organizations. This is especially true when these organizations are seeking funds to start new programs and to expand existing ones. In making this point, I am also saying that the charitable gifts of individuals will remain as the predominant source of regular, operating support for non-profit charitable organizations. My experience tells me that foundations tend to be more interested in new exciting programs and the enhancement of existing, highly successful programs. There are exceptions to this, of course, in that some foundations are very comfortable in making grants to the same organizations and programs year after year. But I believe that such funding practices are few and far between.

The primary objective of this chapter is to "de-mystify" the grant writing process, so that staff and volunteer leaders of non-profit charitable organizations will see it as an achievable adjunct to their total fundraising programs and as something that they can do without the necessity of hiring professional grant writers to do it. I say this here because over the years, both in non-profit organizations and in the classroom, I have come upon a lot of fear and anxiety about making application to foundations. There is no need for this. Grant applications are relatively simple and straightforward things to do. I am not trying to undercut the business of professional grant writers. There is still ample need for them when there is not the time or inclination in non-profit organizations to get the grant writing done. But I am trying to encourage the professional and volunteer staffs of these organizations to not shy away from engaging in the grant writing process simply because they fear that they won't do it right.

With these thoughts in mind, the chapter will proceed ahead as follows. First, I will introduce the legal basis of foundations. Then, I will mention and define the three most common kinds of foundations to which non-profit organizations are likely to apply. Third, I will discuss the importance of doing sufficient research before applying to foundations. Fourth, I will go through the specific steps of the grant application process.

Legal Basis of Foundations

Foundations are non-profit charitable organizations themselves and have from the IRS a 501 (c)(3) status as well. But they are set up and function differently than the non-profit organizations that have been discussed so far in this book. Foundations are established to provide funds for other non-profit charitable organizations through a process of grants. In fact, most of them are required by law to give away at least 5% of the total funds they have each year. If they do not do this, they place their 501(c)(3) status in jeopardy. And this tax status is vital to Foundations because, without it, the donors to these charitable organizations, who are frequently their founders, will not receive a tax deduction for their donations and, thus, will have much less incentive to establish the foundations in the first place or to maintain them once they are established.

This leads to an interesting legal fact about foundations. Donors to foundations receive a tax deduction at the point in time of their donation, even though their funds are not yet being put to use for a charitable purpose. But their donation is irrevocable, and, for this reason and because their funds – or at least the earnings off of them – are destined to be used for a charitable purpose at some point in the future, the IRS allows the tax deduction right away. In this way, the IRS is promoting the existence of foundations as positive forces in our society.

Three Kinds of Foundations

There are three principal kinds of foundations from which non-profit charitable organizations are likely to apply for grants. They are independent, corporate, and community. **Independent Foundations** are the most common. Individuals or families, with their inherited or acquired wealth, usually establish independent foundations. (This is why they are sometimes known as family foundations.) Oftentimes these same people and/or perhaps their children, friends, and associates serve on the foundation Board of Directors and decide upon how the funds are to be invested and the grants to be made. Frequently these foundations, although they may start out quite small, may grow to considerable size over time because their investments regularly generate much more than the 5% they are required to give away each year. Many examples of independent foundations can be found in almost any city or town of even modest size in this country.

Corporate Foundations are established by businesses as a regular way to support the charitable organizations that provide community service in the respective market areas of the businesses. In other words, if these corporations sell their products or services in a defined local area, their foundations will tend to give grants only in that local area. However, if they sell their products or services nationally or internationally, then their foundations will make grants to organizations in a corresponding much wider area. Enhancement of profit – and rightly so – is still very much in the purview of a corporate foundation as it goes about doing good things.

A corporate foundation must be established as a separate legal entity from the corporation itself. There can be overlap of board membership to some degree, as long as there is a legal separation of the two boards and the funds are not intermingled. The foundation board membership is usually appointed by the corporate board and composed of its own members, company executives, and other employees.

In regard to the regular operation of corporate foundations, most are supported through annual budgets proposed by the foundation board and approved by the corporate board. And, just as for the independent foundations, once the corporation places funds in its foundation and a tax deduction is taken, the transfer of funds is irrevocable. Corporate foundations are also readily recognizable within the community because they carry the name of their parent companies. For example, the corporate foundation for the Western Union Company is called the Western Union Foundation.

Community Foundations are rapidly growing in size and number in this country. They are usually established by a group of several donors who agree to pool their funds for both investment and grant making reasons. This frees the individual donor from the burden of going through the legal steps of establishing an independent foundation on his or her own and from the challenges associated with making good investment decisions and reviewing grant applications properly and professionally. There is a resulting economy of scale that brings benefits to all involved, both donors and recipient organizations.

The typical community foundation is organized and established by a group of citizens in a city or town, and this group may or not be people with the wealth needed to get the new organization on a solid financial footing right away. If the group does not have the wealth required, it may agree to conduct community fundraising to acquire the needed funds and/or to seek out the needed funds from others who may have the required wealth. Most community foundations actually maintain a constant fundraising program, and this makes them quite different from both independent and corporate foundations. As a result, some community foundations have become very large over time. For example, the Denver Foundation, which has been around for a long time and is very well established, now has an endowment of around $600 million. And most of these dollars have been obtained in relatively recent years through a very aggressive fundraising program. As another example, the Westminster Legacy Foundation, also in Colorado, is only about six years old. I am privileged to serve on its Board of Directors. We are constantly in a fundraising mode, have only been moderately successful at it, but are proud of the fact that we have now given grants totaling over $150,000 to improve the quality of life in out city.

I have noticed two relatively recent developments in the community foundation arena that have had a huge impact on their capability to make a positive difference in the grant-making world. The first is the huge growth in **donor advised funds**. Individuals or families establish these funds by deciding to give a sum of money irrevocably to a community foundation, receive a tax deduction for the donation, allow the foundation to invest those funds, and then advise the foundation as to when, to which charitable cause, and how much of a contribution to make from their funds. These funds remain separate from the general endowments in community foundations, but they have swelled the dollars available for grants immensely.

The second recent development are the new, instantly strong community foundations resulting from the **sale of non-profit institutions to for-profit companies**. Such sales have become relatively common in many communities in the United States. For example, during the past several years, two non-profit, religion sponsored hospitals in Denver were sold to for-profit medical management companies for large amounts of money. In both instances, the Boards of the two hospitals decided to transfer the proceeds of these sales into new community foundations, now called the Colorado Trust and the Rose Community Foundation, which are among the most generously endowed foundations in the State of Colorado.

Researching Foundations

The number one reason why grant applications end up being rejected by foundations is that they are sent to the wrong foundation in the first place. And, to my way of thinking, this is inexcusable. It is inexcusable because there is extensive information about every foundation that can be accessed through research. Therefore, the first step – and perhaps the most important one – is to determine what is the most appropriate foundation to which an application should be sent for this particular organization or program.

This task of determination takes time, but it is easy. This is especially so because all information about each foundation that an applicant needs to know is readily available. All foundations, because they are 501(c)(3) organizations, are required to file the form 990 to the IRS each year. And, as was learned in the first part of this text on financial management, the form 990 is a public document that must by law be made available to any interested party. But we do not even have to bother to research these original documents. Other helpful organizations do this for us. These same organizations do even more for us. They gather information on foundations that it is not even included on the form 990's of these foundations. For example, in Colorado there is an organization that is called the Community Resource Center. Each year it publishes a directory of all Colorado foundations that is available both in written form and on line (www.crcamerica.org). This directory contains the following data on each foundation: total assets, names of officers and trustees, examples of current grants, amounts of those grants, areas of interest, granting and review cycles, and application procedures. Most States have published directories like this. And, at the national level, organizations like the Foundation Center and the Chronicle of Philanthropy frequently publish helpful information on foundations throughout the country, especially the larger ones.

Now that we know where to do our research, what questions need to be addressed? First of all, the non-profit organization needs to identify foundations that are used to funding – and, more importantly, want to fund – organizations that are like it. For example, if the organization provides services for seniors, it is futile to consider applying to a foundation that states explicitly or implicitly (that is, through its granting decisions) that it is only interested in funding programs for children. In like manner, it is also futile to request a grant for a program beyond the geographic area of the stated interest of a particular foundation. In addition, the organization needs to find out if a particular foundation will consider funding general operating costs, if that is what is needed.

Of special importance is to learn about the appropriate amount to ask for from a specific foundation. Some foundations have clear dollar averages of grant amounts, while others consider applications in a wide range. And I have found that most foundations are not willing to fund the total amount needed for a particular program or non-profit organization. They tend not to want to be a "Lone Ranger" in this regard. They like to see evidence that other funders and other sources of support are involved. But, again, remember what was stated in the beginning of this chapter: "When you know one foundation, you know one foundation."

The good news about research on foundations – and I have had this verified over and over again by the foundation representatives that speak in my classes – is that, if adequate research is done, if the application is directed to an appropriate foundation, if the preferred application procedures are followed (I will talk about these later on in this chapter.), and if the amount requested is in the proper range, then the non-profit charitable organization has a 50% to 60% chance of the application being funded. It seems to me that these are pretty good odds and make the process well worth the effort.

Application Procedures

There are seven steps that come to mind when making the actual application to a foundation, which has been determined to be an appropriate target through the research process.

Step 1: Make an initial contact: It is highly recommended to make some initial contact with the foundation by a one-page letter (time permitting) or by telephone or e-mail. This initial contact should describe briefly the purpose and the amount of the proposed grant request and should ask about their appropriateness. A positive response to this initial inquiry is no guarantee of funding, of course. But such a response can provide assurance that the proposal is of some interest to the foundation. And, if the response is in the negative, the charitable organization is prevented from doing a lot of unnecessary and useless work. This contact is also an opportunity to verify the desired application format, deadlines, and any other important information.

Step 2: Use the preferred format: Most foundations are very clear about the format they wish all applicants to follow. This is a very important issue. In fact, when I ask the foundation representatives who regularly appear in my classes what is their number one complaint about the applications they receive, they most often reply that their directions on format are simply not followed. In other words, certain requested information is not provided, other information is provided that is not requested, or the narrative is too long or too short.

This issue is being made much easier these days as more and more foundations have developed and are using a common grant application format. For example, in Colorado, representatives of several foundations have agreed upon the "Colorado Common Grant Application." This makes it much easier for applicants to provide similar information to several different foundations and allows the foundations themselves to receive comparable information from several different applicants. But, even if a particular foundation indicates that it will accept a common application format, it may also request additional specific information or request not to receive certain information included in the common format. These specific requests can and should be verified in the initial contact.

Step 3: Write a cover letter: Whether requested or not, I always recommend that a brief, one-page cover letter be attached to the completed application. Such a letter gives the applicant organization the opportunity to point out to the foundation the most significant information contained in the application. In class at this point, I often draw the parallel to a professional job application, where the cover letter gives the job applicant the best opportunity to highly personalize his or her application and make a forceful and specific case for employment with that particular employer. In like manner, the cover letter to a foundation should summarize all the salient points of the total application, such as the mission of the applicant organization, the "fit" between this mission and the goals of the foundation itself, the specific reasons for the required funding, and the amount of that funding. It needs to state clearly and succinctly exactly why the foundation **should** provide the needed funding.

Step 4: Follow the "4 C's" of grant writing: The total application, especially the narrative, needs to be clear, concise, compelling, and comprehensive. Being **clear** in this context means that the foundation representatives should never be left with a question about what is meant or intended by the applicant. That is why several people in the applicant organization need to review the application draft before it is finalized and submitted. Avoid all jargon and eliminate other methods of expression that are not generally understood. This clarity objective should carry over to the program budget where narrative explanations are added for any items that are not readily understood.

Being **concise** applies first to sentence and paragraph structure. Short sentences and paragraphs are good; too many long sentences and paragraphs are bad. It also applies to overall length. Most preferred application formats that I have seen request that narratives be limited to only three to five pages. Many non-profit professionals find this requirement to be difficult, primarily because they are proud of their charitable organizations and want to make sure that the application reviewers fully understand everything about the organization's important work. If this brevity requirement proves to be troublesome in a particular instance, then I recommend that the grant writer compose a first draft with everything that he or she thinks should be included, even if the required length is exceeded. Then the writer can seek the advice of others in the organization about what can be eliminated or shortened to reach the required length.

Being **compelling** in the grant application is perhaps the most important concept of all. By this I mean giving the foundation truly significant reasons to grant the request for funds. In this context, the point made much earlier in this text about fundraising being a "voluntary exchange among people" needs to be kept in mind. This applies to foundation fundraising as well. Foundations should receive something in return for their grants, too. Therefore, the grant writer needs to state clearly and forcefully that the funding of this particular organization or program meets the goals and objectives of the foundation itself. Only in this way will the foundation conclude that it is "compelled" to respond positively to the request. Certainly other considerations make the application compelling also – considerations like the quality of the organization's service and staff, the urgent needs of the clients, and so on. Nonetheless, what research tells us about the specific objectives of each foundation must be given major emphasis in grant requests.

Finally, being **comprehensive** in grant applications needs to be defined by the foundations themselves. In other words, the application will only meet the comprehensive requirement if it contains all the information requested by the foundations in their specific guidelines. Foundations are few and far between that will give us time and opportunity to re-submit information that should have been submitted in the first place. More than likely, an incomplete application will be dismissed outright, given the fact that not all applications can be funded anyway. In other words, being comprehensive means not to give the foundation any excuse to not fund the proposal. Remember what I stated above in Step 2. Foundation representatives themselves have indicated in my classes that the most frequent reason for their rejections are applications that are incomplete.

Step 5: Make personal contact: At some point in the application process and whenever it is possible, it is almost always a good idea to make some personal contact with a representative of the foundation by telephone or in person. This may be done during the initial contact phase as described above in Step 1. And/or it can be done at almost any other point in the process, for example, during the time that the application is being prepared to ask an appropriate question or when the completed application is submitted. Such contact serves to establish a personal relationship with the foundation, and, as has been seen in all other methods of fundraising, a personal relationship is an important key to success.

But who should be contacted? This is a significant question, because it is easy to make a mistake in this regard. My strong recommendation is to make contact first with the professional staff of the foundation – at least when and if the foundation has such staff, as more and more of them do in these days. My experience and the unanimous response of foundation representatives in my courses indicate that calls and other communications with staff persons are always welcome and encouraged. They would much rather help with our applications during the process of their preparation than have to reject or send them back to us later on. But I did say above that it is easy to make a mistake in this regard. For example, let's say that a board member of the non-profit organization knows a board member of the foundation and wishes to contact that person directly about the application and to bypass the foundation staff. Such a tactic is often seen as "pressure" by the foundation and not appreciated at all. Therefore, I strongly suggest that, before such a tactic is employed, the first contact should always be made with the foundation staff. At that point, the organization can inform the staff person about the friendship between the two board members and ask if such contact would be appropriate. The organization will often find that there is a strong preference among the board members of the foundation that they not be contacted in this way. Oftentimes that is one of the primary reasons why staff people have been hired in the first place.

Step 6: Be prepared for a site visit: Many foundations, especially those who have professional staff, will visit non-profit charitable organizations or programs as an important step in their evaluation process before they make a decision about funding. This may be a nervous time for the applicant organization, but it need not be. First of all, the organization should be encouraged by such site visits, primarily because they most probably would not happen if the foundation was not giving serious consideration to the proposal. And, secondly, I have found that people with a sincere interest in our programs conduct these visits in a supportive fashion. The foundations representatives are not looking for reasons to **not fund** the organization's programs. Rather they are simply trying to verify some information that may not be totally clear to them in the application and to gain an overall impression of the organization and its people and services, especially if this is the first time that they have had contact with the organization. I believe that the foundation representatives are more likely to be looking for reasons **to fund** the programs!

Given this understanding, how should the non-profit organization prepare for a site visit? And there will be time to prepare, because no foundation would attempt a "surprise" by dropping by unannounced. I would start by simply asking the foundation representatives what and whom they would like to see and respond accordingly. If the foundation staff persons will conduct the visit, I would correspondingly have the organization's staff meet with them. In the same way, if foundation board members are making the visits or are included, I would include members of the board, preferably the Board Chair. It is important to alert everyone throughout the organization that a site visit is happening and that it is significant. But I would not add to the nervousness that is already naturally there in the organization. Rather, I would encourage everyone to conduct "business as usual" and to be friendly and open to any interruption of normal activity that may transpire. Keep in mind that the foundation representatives are now friends who believe in what the organization is doing – or they would not be making the site visit at all.

Step 7: Say thanks regardless: An expression of gratitude is in order whatever the outcome of the application process may be. Whether the foundation supports the application totally, partially, or not at all, the charitable organization should express thanks for the consideration given to the application. This is obvious when the response is a positive one. But it should be equally as obvious when the response is not so positive or even totally negative. In these latter instances, the expression of gratitude re-affirms the professionalism of the charitable organization, builds a positive relationship with the foundation for future applications, and provides the opportunity to request information on how the application could have been made stronger. I believe that most foundation representatives are most willing to provide good advice for the future, which not only will be helpful when the organization applies again to their foundations, but also when it applies to other foundations.

Bullet Summary

♦ Foundations present a significantly growing source of funding for non-profit charitable organizations.

♦ Most charitable organizations have the "in house" capability to be successful in the grant writing process, although contracting with professional grant writers can be helpful in some instances.

♦ Foundations are non-profit charitable organizations, but they are not established to provide programs and services themselves, but to support through grants the programs and services of other charitable organizations.

♦ There are three distinctly different kinds of foundations, namely, independent, corporate, and community foundations. Each is funded differently and usually requires different application procedures.

♦ Not only is each kind of foundation different, but also each individual foundation is quite different in its funding priorities, amount of grants, geographic limitations, application procedures and deadlines, and other important matters. Therefore, it is essential to conduct extensive research to identify the particular foundations that may be the most appropriate for specific organizations and applications.

♦ There are seven recommended steps to follow in making application to foundations. These are:

1. Make an initial contact with the targeted foundation.

2. Use the format preferred by the particular foundation.

3. Write a brief cover letter that highlights the application for the foundation.

4. Follow the "4 C's" of grant writing by being clear, concise, compelling, and comprehensive.

5. Make personal contact with the foundation at some point in the process.

6. Be prepared for a site visit by foundation representatives.

7. Say thanks afterwards, regardless of the outcome of the application.

Conclusion

Hopefully, this chapter has successfully "de-mystified" the grant writing process, so that raising money from foundations can take its appropriate and important place in the development programs of non-profit charitable organizations. This chapter also completes Part B of the book on the elements of a comprehensive fundraising program in a non-profit charitable organization. I emphasize again the point that a fundraising program must be truly diversified, so that the successful pursuit of the organization's mission does not become overly dependent on only one or two sources of funding and so that it can retain its independence as it attempts to implement its worthwhile goals whatever they may be.

Suggested Reading

Ciconte and Jacob, op.cit., pp. 197-224.

EPILOGUE

Non-profit charitable organizations, if they are to continue to thrive in the United States and to expand effectively into many other countries – as they are at a very rapid rate – must operate with some important principles in mind. If they do not, they will lose the trust of the public that they depend upon not only for their financial support, but also for their client bases that provide the very reasons for their existence. These principles are:

1. Non-profit charitable organizations are ultimately **accountable** to the public and can only be truly accountable if they are fully **transparent** in their financial records and act as **fiduciaries** of the assets they possess.

2. Volunteer Boards of Directors have the ultimate **legal responsibility** for the well-being and mission achievement of non-profit charitable organizations.

3. Professional staffs of charitable organizations **implement** the policies of the Boards of Directors and **work in partnership** with the Boards to achieve the missions of the organizations.

4. The financially strongest charitable organizations direct the majority of their fundraising efforts to **individual donors** with whom they have established personal relationships.

5. Non-profit charitable organizations will succeed if their **missions** are perceived to be worthwhile by the public; if they have **responsible Boards** and **competent staffs**; if they conduct **diversified, comprehensive fundraising programs** that not only provide sufficient operating funds, but also adequate financial reserves; and if they produce and distribute accurate **reports on the use of the funds** entrusted to their care.

6. The operation of non-profit charitable organizations is a **tremendous asset** to the United States and, if expanded appropriately and with sensitivity, can become a great **gift to the world** from the American people.

Let's return to the primary title of this book: **"Managing and Raising Money that is Not Your Own."** I believe that this phrase adequately and precisely summarizes all that is written in this text. Yes, the money that non-profit charitable organizations already have, as well as the additional money they seek to acquire through their fundraising efforts, **is not their own.** The money belongs to the public, to donors, and to their clients. It has been entrusted to non-profit organizations for one purpose only – to carry out their respective missions. If the organizations do not manage this money well and do not use it efficiently and effectively for their missions, they will violate the bond of trust they have with their constituents. This violation may not be forgiven for a very long time and, at a minimum, will make their fundraising efforts much more difficult than they need to be. This violation may also lead to something much more serious – the end of a non-profit charitable organization, no matter how important and how needed the fulfillment of it's mission may be.

With these thoughts in mind, I now close with a challenge to all of you who are on the Boards of Directors of non-profit charitable organizations, who are among the executive or management staffs of these organizations, or who aspire to be in these positions in the future. Your dedication to the betterment of society and our world is obvious, because you would not be in – or want to be in – these positions unless you were so dedicated. But you will never achieve the goals of your dedication – your missions – unless, by following the principles enumerated in the beginning of this epilogue, you **raise** the essential resource of money effectively and then **manage** it efficiently, doing both with the full realization that this resource **is not your own.** So do it! If you do, you will succeed – and the world, indeed, **will** be a better place.

LaVergne, TN USA
17 March 2011
220620LV00002B/3-8/P